# The Italian Immigrant Experience: Between Black and White

EDITED BY
Vincent Bocchimuzzo
Elena Daniele
Anthony Julian Tamburri

JOHN D. CALANDRA ITALIAN AMERICAN INSTITUTE
QUEENS COLLEGE, THE CITY UNIVERSITY OF NEW YORK

STUDIES IN ITALIAN AMERICANA
VOLUME 17

John D. Calandra Italian American Institute
Queens College, CUNY
25 West 43rd Street, 17th floor
New York, NY 10036

ISBN 978-1-939323-14-9
Library of Congress Control Number: 2024945778

# CONTENTS

# Preface

VINCENT BOCCHIMUZZO
ELENA DANIELE
ANTHONY JULIAN TAMBURRI

> Why is the death of the ordinary man a wretched, chilling
> thing which we turn from, while the death of the hero,
> always tragic, warms us with a sense of quickened life?
> —Edith Hamilton, *The Greek Way*

After the Civil War and during Reconstruction thousands of Italians, largely from Sicily, emigrated to New Orleans to find work that became available after the abolition of slavery. Many Sicilian immigrants settled in New Orleans in the lower French Quarter that became known as Little Palermo. In his book *The Italians*, Luigi Barzini reminds us: "Sicilian Immigrants to the United States found themselves surrounded by an alien and hostile society. They had to cope with incomprehensible language, puzzling customs, rigid laws, and what they considered an oppressive regime. They clung to what could give them protection and comfort, the Church, family, and their ways" (272).

The most infamous example of violence against the Italian community was the lynching and murder of eleven immigrants from Italy by a vigilante mob in 1891 for their alleged role in the killing of New Orleans Police Chief David Hennessy. One of the largest mass lynchings in American history, the incident reflected the times during which Italian immigrants to the United States were not considered white and were the subject of discrimination and hate crimes.[1]

According to the recent 2020 report from the Equal Justice Initiative, the documented lynchings of Black people in the United States reached a staggering number of almost 6,500 between 1865 and 1950. In turn, the African American community in New Orleans and beyond has of course borne the brunt of discrimination and the violent hate crime of lynching.

On September 23 and 24, 2022, Tulane University and the John D. Calandra Italian American Institute collaborated in presenting a symposium titled "The Italian Immigrant Experience: Between Black and White." The symposium was held in New Orleans, on the Tulane campus. The symposium featured scholars who study the Italian American and the Black experiences in New Orleans as well as throughout the United States. This book is a compilation of the papers presented at the symposium.

At the forefront of organizing this event was a desire to provide students and the public with historical knowledge regarding the Italian immigrant experience during the late nineteenth century. The speakers who presented their papers are among the many scholars who have dedicated their lives to researching these topics, and they adhere, as well, to criteria of historical accuracy. This was tantamount to complying with Dean Anthony Julian Tamburri's plea in his most recent book, *A Politics of [Self-]Omission*: "Anything short of solid knowledge of these facts and how to relate them to other phenomena is simply not acceptable" (75).

As the author and critic Robert Viscusi implored us, we must actively engage and preserve our own culture and history, or we risk allowing others to shape the narrative in ways that may not reflect our true identity. It is crucial to take ownership of our heritage to ensure it is represented accurately and authentically. He articulated such notions in his "three rules of IAWA (Italian American Writers Association): "Read one another. Write or be written. Buy our books."[2]

• • •

One of the initial questions is, Why is such a symposium needed? In reviewing the initial wave of Italian immigration during the late nineteenth century, the immigrants' heart-wrenching experiences, and the atrocities that the African American community was facing, it made sense to explore the commonalities overlapping the different experiences of these two communities. A symposium of this nature thus calls into question, as well, the notion of interethnic collaboration. As many of us would agree, ethnicity is a sociopolitical construct, and as such it differentiates only insofar as it points out the major characteristics of one group as compared to those of another. These differences, moreover, may also have corollaries and analogs in certain characteristics of other ethnic groups. Let us not forget that biology is different from sociology and that one's cellular make-up—i.e., his/her race—does not necessarily override one's long-term social and cultural experiences—her/his ethnicity.

In his 1974 study *Ethnic Alienation*, Patrick Gallo spoke to the need for a partnership between ethnic groups. In closing his ground-breaking study of the political behavior of three generations of Italian Americans and the possibility of ethnic groups sharing political power, he stated, "What is needed is an alliance of whites and Blacks, white-collar and blue-collar workers, based on mutual need and interdependence and hence an alliance of political participation." Namely, the us *and* them, not the us *against* them. "But," Gallo continues, "before this can realistically come to pass, a number of ethnic groups have to develop in-group organization, identity, and unity." And here Viscusi's notion of the "group narrative" comes to mind. Finally, Gallo concludes, "Italian-Americans may prove to be [one of many] vital ingredient[s] in not only forging that alliance but in serving as the cement that will hold our urban centers together" (Gallo, 209).[3]

• • •

Reverend Frank Williams delivered one of two keynote addresses at the Tulane symposium and reminded us that surviving is not just the breadth of one's body: it is the identity in one's heart. This identity blossoms via a multigenerational mission not merely to survive, but eventually to thrive. In examining the church's role in slavery, he reminded us that the church made slavery a civil and political issue, although it was never confronted as a moral issue. Williams's words resonate with all who are discriminated against today. In his closing remarks, he reminded us not to be intoxicated with early successes, as this is a multigenerational struggle.

In August 1959, Italian American poet, translator, novelist, and humanist Professor Joseph Tusiani began a correspondence with Dr. Martin Luther King Jr during which Dr. King wrote to Prof. Tusiani that the problems facing our world in the area of human relations are chiefly moral; they are not economic and political but moral. Sixty-three years later, at the Tulane Symposium, our keynote speaker Reverend Williams echoed the same thought.

Our second keynote address was by John Gennari. His comprehensive analysis places the controversial Original Dixieland Jazz Band within the complex intersection of music, race, class, and migration in both New Orleans and the broader United States, emphasizing transnational influences. His scholarly examination delves into Italian American cultural practices and their portrayal, as highlighted by the symposium theme "between black and white." Gennari compellingly illustrates how the band's whiteness afforded them significant advantages in securing performances, particularly at prestigious venues in a segregated America and in Europe. Moreover, he underscores their pivotal role in early jazz histories, which historically marginalized African American contributions.

The two keynote addresses bracketed three keen presentations. Jessica Barbata Jackson presented an overview of how Italian immigrants passed between racial communities: they moved through the society of the time as both white Southerners and people of color. Mark Reid considered Spike Lee's interethnic depiction in film of both a loving and antagonistic relationship between African Americans and Italian Americans. In so doing, he demonstrated how Lee's film and Roberto Rossellini's 1946 *Paisà* "contribute to a bid for compassion during internecine historical moments when war and social chaos rule society" (page 65). George De Stefano, in turn, provided an examination of Sicilian dominance of the French Quarter's entertainment venues, the involvement of organized crime in them, and how the respective experiences of white and Black New Orleanians differed greatly.

In addition to the three presentations, each keynote address received a written response: Fred Gardaphé examined differences between religion built on accepted fate and religion emerging from a struggle for freedom in his response to Frank Williams's address; in turn, Joseph Sciorra discussed the ongoing engagement with Black/White history via public monuments in New Orleans as articulated in John Gennari's keynote.

This book reflects the continuing effort between Tulane University and the John D. Calandra Italian American Institute to present the facts as they are and, further, to illuminate the public in the continuing search for the truth in the Italian/American immigrant experience between Black and White. In our desire to paint as best we might an accurate picture of the times, Giovanni Schiavo comes to mind. In underscoring the importance of acquiring the requisite knowledge in portraying our past, he stated that we should spend the time "digging and digging, without expectation of any reward, except the feeling of doing some good." The "feeling of doing some good" (3)—and not, as seems the wont of many, "*fare lo spaccone*" (trans., act like a bigshot) regardless of one's lack of expertise—should be our end goal.

## Acknowledgment

The editors wish to express their heartfelt, *caloroso grazie* to Siân Gibby for her continued copyediting and proofing of this volume.

## Notes

[1] The largest lynching on record in the United States took place in Los Angeles on October 24, 1871. In all, nineteen Chinese were killed; fifteen by hanging, four by gunshot (Grad).

[2] Iawa.net/history/.

[3] We borrow here from Tamburri 2023.

## Works Cited

Anonymous. "The History of IAWA." *Italian American Writers Association*. www.iawa.net. Accessed July 24, 2024.

Barzini, Luigi. 1964. *The Italians*. New York: Atheneum Books.

"EJI's Reconstruction in America Report Changes Picture of Lynching in America." 2020. *Equal Justice Initiative*. Montgomery, Alabama. https://eji.org/news/reconstruction-in-america-report-changes-picture-of-lynching-in-america/.

Gallo, Patrick. 1974. *Ethnic Alienation: The Italian-Americans.* Madison, NJ: Fairleigh Dickinson University Press.

Grad, Shelby. 2021. "The Racist Massacre That Killed 10% 0f L.A.'S Chinese Population and Brought Shame to The City." *Los Angeles Times*. March 18. https://www.latimes.com/california/story/2021-03-18/reflecting-los-angeles-chinatown-massacre-after-atlanta-shootings.

Hamilton, Edith. 1930. *The Greek Way* W.W. Norton and Company.

Schiavo, Giovanni. 1976. *The Italians in America Before the Revolution.* New York: The Vigo Press.

Tamburri, Anthony Julian. 2022. *A Politics of [Self-]Omission. he Italian/American Challenge in a Post-George Floyd Age.* Arcane.

Tamburri, Anthony Julian. 2023. "Italian Americans and African Americans 50 Years Later: What Might We Do?" *Teaching Italian Language and Culture Annual*: 55–64. https://tilca.qc.cuny.edu/.

Viscusi Robert. 1990. "Breaking the Silence: Strategic Imperatives for an Italian American Culture." *Voices in Italian Americana* 1.1: 1–13.

Viscusi, Robert. 2006. *Buried Caesars and Other Secrets of Italian American Writing.* Albany, NY: SUNY Press.

# Pursuing Liberation: A Socio-Spiritual Journey toward Freedom

FRANK I. WILLIAMS

## INTRODUCTION

In a conversation with a friend, I was asked, "Why are African Americans in the predicament they are in? What did we [and by *we* she meant Black people in general] do in history to warrant such treatment?" Her question emerged out of a larger conversation about a Black man who was arrested while doing some mundane task as a favor for his neighbor in their own neighborhood and a string of other similar occurrences that became criminalized. Her question also came from a place of pain and perplexity that all too often reflects the reality of Black life in the United States of America. In his book *The Cross and the Lynching Tree*, James Cone (2011), the founder of Black Liberation Theology, recalls a similar query. "If God loves black people, why then do we suffer so much? That was my question as a child; that is still my question" (Cone 2011, 154), he wrote. The weight of these questions traveled a long history that included the cumulative impact of betrayal, enslavement, rejection, trauma, and psychological mutilation. It requires an extraordinary amount of resilience for a people to survive such torment. Recovery would be a multigenerational journey that demands household, religious, and civic commitment to the personal and systemic changes needed to move generations from surviving to thriving; and by *surviving*, I refer not merely to the breath in one's body, but also to the identity in one's heart. This identity is commonly rooted in one's place of origin—be that based on cultural affiliation, place of birth, or national heritage. However, I postulate that the multilayered history of enslavement, forced relocation, and racism left a scar so deep only God could redeem and restore from that kind of brokenness and the disempowering effect of isolation and fear that it produced.

## THE STONY ROAD: A BRIEF HISTORICAL SKETCH, PART 1

The descendants of Africans brought to the Americas as enslaved persons are a unique people in terms of their history. In the book *From Slavery to Freedom: A History of Negro Americans* (Sixth Edition), authors and historians John Hope Franklin and Alfred A. Moss Jr. pointed out that, "Slavery was widespread during the earliest known history of Africa as well as of other continents. . . . Slavery in the Greek and Roman empires is well known" (Franklin and Moss 1988, 27). Among those populations, "the opportunities for education and cultural advancement were . . . opened up to slaves. It was not unusual to find in that class persons possessing a degree of intelligence and training not usually associated with slaves" (27–28). Robert Liston in his book *Slavery in America: The History of Slavery* affirmed the same: "Many slaves of Egypt, Greece, and Rome were educated and rose to positions of authority and power" (Liston 1970).

Specifically, concerning slavery in Africa, Franklin wrote, "Slaves in these lands were essentially servants, and the extent of the demand for them depended in a large measure on the wealth of the potential masters. Slavery was, therefore, a manifestation of wealth, and the institution showed little of the harshness and severity that it possessed in areas where it was itself the foundation on which wealth was built" (Franklin and Moss 1988, 28). African history scholar Paul E. Lovejoy does note in his work *Transformations in Slavery: A History of Slavery in Africa* (Third Edition) that in African societies, "slavery functioned on the edge of society. There were some slaves who had failed to pay debts, been convicted of crimes, charged with sorcery, seized in war, or transferred as compensation for damages" (Lovejoy 2012, 44). According to Lovejoy slavery was usually initiated by violence of some kind but was maintained on a small scale by wealthy masters and kinship networks (13). He continues:

> The existence of slaves in [African] societies that emphasized kinship and dependency permitted their integration into a vast network of international slavery. This integration probably stretched far back into the past, but only for those areas closest to the Mediterranean basin, the Persian Gulf, and the Indian Ocean. By the eighth, ninth, and tenth centuries, the Islamic world had become the heir to this long tradition of slavery, continuing the pattern of incorporating black slaves from Africa into the societies north of the Sahara and along the shores of the Indian Ocean. The Muslim states of this period interpreted the ancient tradition of slavery in accordance with their new religion, but many uses for slaves were the same as before—slaves were used in the military, administration, and domestic service. (15)

While "slavery is probably as old as civilization, until the white man came to Africa, slavery was usually an adjunct of war" (Liston 1970, 21). However, the enslavement of Africans for and in the Americas was not "an adjunct of war." The European countries that initiated and developed what became the transatlantic slave trade were driven by an increasing appetite for economic power and political expansion. Franklin described this ambition as follows:

> It was the forces let loose by the Renaissance and the Commercial Revolution that created the modern institution of slavery and the slave trade. The Renaissance gave to man a new kind of freedom—the freedom to pursue those ends that would be most beneficial to his soul and body. It developed into such a passionate search that it resulted in the destruction of long-established practices and beliefs and even the destruction of rights of others to pursue the same ends for their own benefit. As W. E. B. Du Bois has pointed out, it was freedom to destroy freedom, the freedom of some to exploit the rights of others. If, then, a man was determined to be free, who was there to tell him that he was not entitled to enslave others? (Franklin and Moss 1988, 28)

This new disposition, coupled with the quest for wealth and global expansion, created a continuous demand for a human workforce for which indentured servitude alone would prove insufficient. By the mid-1400s the Portuguese, in search of gold in the West African coastal territories, began buying and selling slaves between African coastal kingdoms and clans. Eventually, some slaves were brought "to southern Europe for employment as domestic servants" (Lovejoy 2012, 36). As the need for labor increased in other regions, by the early to mid-1500s, European countries that were already trading goods on the West African coast began capturing, buying, and/or exporting African people as chattel slave labor to their "newly discovered" territories in other parts of the world. Thus, the transatlantic slave trade was born.

Liston provided further perspective that connects how the "forces let loose by the Renaissance" facilitated the establishment of slavery as an international transatlantic business. He wrote: "The big boom in the slave business came with the discovery of America, but even then, a quarter of a century was required before New World settlers realized that Africans were the 'ideal' slaves" (1970, 25). Liston also noted that, "while an effort was made, particularly by the English colonists, to recruit white labor from Europe as indentured servants . . . this system did not relieve the labor shortage. . . . Finally, the Europeans, as white Christians, could not be treated harshly and driven to perform [the] infinite amount of work there was to do in the New World" (26). Additionally, according to Franklin, "Englishmen began to ask themselves why they should be concerned with white servants when blacks presented so few of the difficulties encountered with the whites. Because of their color, Negros could easily be apprehended. . . .

Negroes, from a pagan land and without exposure to the ethical ideals of Christianity, could be handled with more rigid methods of discipline and could be morally and spiritually degraded for the sake of stability on the plantation" (Franklin and Moss 1988, 32).

Prior to this, "ancient slavery had little if anything to do with race" (Liston 1970, 21). And so the race-based transatlantic slave trade grew with a seemingly inexhaustible supply of Black bodies being exported from Western Africa to develop the New World colonies.

While Christianity was not new to the African continent,[1] it was, according to some historians, not prevalent among the enslaved populations. Franklin emphasized that Christianity became "entrenched" in North Africa well before the seventh century, but "in West Africa . . . from which the great bulk of slaves was secured, Christianity was practically unknown until the Portuguese began to plant missions in the area in the sixteenth century" (Franklin and Moss 1988, 21). Some West Africans who were exposed to Christianity at that time saw it as a strange and contradictory religion because they could not reconcile its teachings with the incompatible behavior of its white practitioners (Franklin and Moss 1988, 21). Slave traders and slaveholders feared that allowing enslaved Africans full access to the Bible could lead to conflicts of interest; thus, baptizing an enslaved Black person could create social and religious implications for which they were not ready. Author and historian Katharine Gerbner, in her book *Christian Slavery: Conversion and Race in the Protestant Atlantic World*, dealt extensively with this crisis from the perspective of life in the Caribbean colonies in the late 1600s, stating: "When enslaved and free blacks sought out and won baptism for themselves and their children, they forced planters to reconsider the relationship between freedom and Protestantism. Could slaves become Christians? Should all Christians be free? And could free black Christians become voters who had the same rights and liberties as European colonists? Protestant planters answered these questions by highlighting whiteness, rather than Christian status, as the primary indicator of mastery and freedom" (Gerbner 2018, 236–237).

Race continued to rise as the distinguishing factor for slaveholders. While conflicting views regarding the enslaved converting to Christianity and being baptized remained prevalent in the New World colonies and territories, one thing was now clear: Enslaved Black Christians and freed Black Christians would not be considered equal to whites. Nevertheless, some slaveholders in the New World allowed enslaved Africans to learn selected portions of the Bible and to attend worship, provided that it reinforced their obedience and they remained in their designated sections.

As enslaved Africans were taught the Bible and experienced conversions to Christianity, they were permitted to form their own religious small groups. The first "sustained" Black congregation on record, the First African Baptist Church, was established by Rev. George Liele in 1778–1779 (Shannon, 2012, 52). Liele was ordained a minister while enslaved in the South, was granted his freedom by his master, and eventually departed for Jamaica (becoming the first known modern-era missionary on record), where he founded churches. Shortly thereafter, Rev. Richard Allen, a slave in the North who was able to purchase his freedom, left the predominantly white Methodist Church after multiple instances of intolerable discrimination, including a group of Black parishioners being pulled from their kneeling posture in prayer and told, "You must get up—you must not kneel here" (Allen 1960, 25) as they were praying in a section where colored people were not allowed. He went on to establish the African Methodist Episcopal (AME) Church in 1816, the first Black Protestant denomination.

After years of mounting pressure from abolitionists, clergy, and antislavery forces, the British ended their involvement in the transatlantic slave trade in 1807 and abolished slavery in 1833 (Hochschild 2005, 309, 346–347). It would be five years later, on August 1, 1838, that colonial slavery would also end. Adam Hochschild, in his book *Bury the Chains: Prophets and Rebels in the Fight to Free an Empire's Slaves*, described a triumphant service that took place in Jamaica as they celebrated the death of slavery in the colony. Referring to slavery, the congregation sang:

> The death-blow is struck—see the monster is dying,
> He cannot survive till the dawn streaks the sky;
> In one single hour, he will prostrate be lying,
> Come, shout o'er the grave where so soon he will lie. (Hochschild 2005, 348)

However, the newly independent United States of America, which now had an ample supply of slave labor, decided that it was economically beneficial to maintain Africans as slaves. At this point, the church in the US was conflicted over the moral implications of slavery. By the 1850s, the North and the South held divergent views on the matter, which were further exacerbated by political and economic conflicts that eventually intensified and led to the Civil War. The Southern states largely supported slavery, and churches in the South continued to view slavery as primarily a sociopolitical issue and not a religious one. Thus, churches depended on laws like the slave codes to inform its position and so justified slavery as a matter of the law (Franklin and Moss 1988, 114). In his book

*The Church and Slavery*, first published in 1857 during the height of this contention, Albert Barnes (at the time a prominent Presbyterian minister) wrote about this conflict, saying that "it is probable that slavery could not be sustained in this land if it were not for the countenance, direct and indirect, of the churches" (1857, 28). Barnes further condemned the inhumanity of this practice within his own religious community:

> There is a deep and growing conviction in the minds of the mass of mankind that slavery violates great laws of our nature; that it is essentially unjust, oppressive, and cruel; that it invades the rights of liberty with which the Author of our being has endowed all human beings; and that, in all the forms in which it has ever existed, it has been impossible to guard it from what its friends and advocates would call "abuses of the system." It is a violation of the first sentiments expressed in our Declaration of Independence, and on which our fathers founded the vindication of their own conduct in an appeal to arms; it is at war with all that a man claims for himself and for his own children; and it is opposed to all the struggles of mankind, in all ages, for freedom. The claims of humanity plead against it. The struggles for freedom everywhere in our world condemn it. (33)

Conversely, some religious slaveholders believed the people they enslaved would never have known the Gospel had they not been enslaved and felt that this spiritual benefit justified the horrors of the institution. Gregory Wills documents this view in his book *Southern Baptist Theological Seminary 1859–2009*: "As an unintended consequence of African slavery, several million Africans were introduced to the gospel of redemption, and a large number of them were converted and redeemed. Basil Manly Jr. wrote that 'their introduction into this country has been, in the providence of God, instrumental in saving more of their race from heathenism, than the united membership of all the churches which foreign missions have planted'" (Wills 2009, 57). It would seem that some Southern Christians used the mandate of Jesus in Matthew 28:18–20,[2] called the Great Commission, to justify the ungodly system of slavery, as long as they taught the enslaved Africans the Bible. As more enslaved persons were taught to read, it became increasingly difficult for slaveholders to suppress certain biblical truths from the Black religious community. Truths that revealed a God who loves justice:

> Psalm 33:4–5 (Christian Standard Bible [CSB]), "For the word of the Lord is right, and all His work is trustworthy. [5] He loves righteousness and justice; the earth is full of the Lord's unfailing love."

Psalm 89:14 (CSB), "Righteousness and justice are the foundation of Your throne; faithful love and truth go before You."

Psalm 72:4 (New King James Version [NKJV]), "He will bring justice to the poor of the people; He will save the children of the needy, and will break in pieces the oppressor."

Proverbs 21:3 (NKJV), "To do righteousness and justice is more acceptable to the Lord than sacrifice."

Micah 6:8 (NKJV), "He has shown you, O man, what *is* good; And what does the Lord require of you but to do justly, to love mercy, and to walk humbly with your God?"

Like their West African ancestors of the sixteenth century, they too began to see the clear contradictions between biblical faith and slaveholder practice. In their struggle to actualize freedom, Black Christians learned that they could look to the God of the Bible as their liberator and summon heaven's intervention on their behalf. Cone described this aspect of their struggle as follows:

> Cut off from their African religious traditions, black slaves were left trying to carve out a religious meaning for their lives with white Christianity as the only resource to work with. They ignored white theology, which did not affirm their humanity, and went straight to stories in the Bible, interpreting them as stories of God siding with little people like them. They identified God's liberation of the poor as the central message of the Bible, and communicated this message in their songs and sermons. (Cone 2011, 118)

While some enslaved Africans adopted Christianity in ways that pleased their slaveholders, inevitably some did so in ways that challenged the moral integrity of owning slaves while claiming Jesus Christ as Lord. An excerpt from the work *African American Religious History: A Documentary Witness*, edited by Milton C. Sernett (1999), illustrates the former. Sernett quotes Jupiter Hammon, the first Black writer to publish in the United States, who communicated an understanding of Christianity that underscored the importance of obedience to one's "master" as an act of obedience to God:

> Now whether it is right, and lawful, in the sight of God, for them to make slaves of us or not, I am certain that while we are slaves, it is our duty to obey our masters, in all their lawful commands, and mind them unless we are bid to do which we know to be sin, or forbidden in God's word. The apostle Paul says,

"Servants be obedient to them that are your master according to the flesh, with fear and trembling in singleness in your heart as unto Christ." . . . It may seem hard for us, if we think our masters wrong in holding us as slaves, to obey in all things, but who of us dare dispute with God! (Sernett 1999, 35–36) [3]

Contrast this with the following excerpts from *Narrative of the Life of Frederick Douglass, An American Slave*. Douglass, who testified that religious slaveholders were "the most cruel," loathed the experience of "belonging to a religious slaveholder," and further despised living near ministers—whom he identified by name as members "in the Reformed Methodist Church" (Douglass 1849, 78). After speaking disparagingly about religious slaveholders and their cruelty, Douglass clarified his position on religion in the appendix of his narrative, distinguishing between what he called "Christianity proper" and slaveholder's Christianity:

What I have said respecting and against religion, I mean strictly to apply to the slaveholding religion of this land, and with no possible reference to Christianity proper; for, between the Christianity of this land and the Christianity of Christ, I recognize the widest possible difference—so wide, that to receive the one as good, pure, and holy, is of necessity to reject the other as bad, corrupt, and wicked. To be the friend of the one, is of necessity to be the enemy of the other. I love the pure, peaceable, and impartial Christianity of Christ: I therefore hate the corrupt, slaveholding, women-whipping, cradle-plundering, partial and hypocritical Christianity of this land. . . . We have men-stealers for ministers, women-whippers for missionaries, and cradle-plunderers for church members. The man who wields the blood-clotted cowskin during the week fills the pulpit on Sunday and claims to be a minister of the meek and lowly Jesus. The man who robs me of my earnings at the end of each week meets me as a class-leader on Sunday morning, to show me the way of life, and the path of salvation. He who sells my sister, for purposes of prostitution, stands forth as the pious advocate of purity. He who proclaims it a religious duty to read the Bible denies me the right of learning to read the name of the God who made me. . . . We see the thief preaching against theft, and the adulterer against adultery. We have men sold to build churches, women sold to support the gospel, and babes sold to purchase Bibles for the poor heathens! all for the glory of God and the good of souls! (118–119) [4]

Douglass's life is evidence that, as a broader scope of biblical content became known to enslaved Black people, there was a clear distinction in how the Bible and the practice of Christianity were understood among the growing Black Christian population versus the slaveholder's brand of Christianity.

The complex moral justification for this form of oppression reached another boiling point during the Civil War when, in 1863 and 1865 respectively, the passing of the Emancipation Proclamation and the Thirteenth Amendment to the US Constitution made slavery illegal in the United States. Cone posited that "Most southern whites were furious at the very idea of granting ex-slaves social, political, and economic freedom" (Cone 2011, 4). They "felt insulted by the suggestion that whites and blacks might work together as equals" (4). This sentiment did not diminish with the conclusion of the Civil War in 1866 (Plante 2015).[5] Instead, the evidence of this sentiment was further strengthened by an increasing defiance with regard to the Thirteenth and Fourteenth (ratified July 9, 1868) Amendments to the US Constitution. The amendments, although they made slavery unconstitutional and granted citizenship (respectively) to Black people, did not end injustice toward the now freed Black population. Moreover, the colluding of multiple white-led religious institutions that shared this sentiment amounted to what history has proven to be an arrogant sin against God. The ideology of white racial supremacy, which was already at work, was now emerging more aggressively. With this new enterprise, an even darker spiritual condition settled across the land, in particular among the Southern states.

THE THORNY TRUTH: A BRIEF HISTORICAL SKETCH, PART 2

Reactions against Reconstruction-era (1865–1877) laws and amendments[6] deepened. White-led churches in America (evidently, but not exclusively, in the South) failed to embrace the new laws that liberated the formerly enslaved population and thereby fully revealed their loyalty to the ideology of the "biological inferiority" of Black persons. In his book *Redeeming the South: Religious Cultures and Racial Identities Among Southern Baptists 1865–1925*, Paul Harvey (1997) wrote about the widely accepted belief that Black people were not just different racially, but created by God to be an inferior race: "That Negroes were created as a separate and inferior race, that black worship consisted of heathenish revelries, that black preachers were unequipped to lead their flocks, and (during Reconstruction, at least) that black churches might become dangerous centers for political organizing—these were fundamental articles of faith held by nearly all white southern Christians after 1865" (Harvey 1997, 33). "During Reconstruction, white southern Baptists prepared for a cultural and political war to defend white supremacy. If violence was necessary to this end, they were prepared to use it" (42). Here the practice of white supremacy did not bend in humility toward Christ, but instead attempted to make God an accomplice in its crimes.

This ideology was likely bolstered by now discredited secular theories like eugenics (using "good" human selection methods to improve human offspring) and polygenism (the theory of multiple origins of human races) (Keel 2013), which invaded the world and made their way into the US by the late 1800s and early 1900s. These ideologies became useful "scientific" tools that fostered racist motivations disguised as a quest for the advancement of the human race. According to a Harvard University Library resource on confronting anti-Black racism titled "Scientific Racism," "One of the most effective tactics used to justify anti-Black racism and white supremacy has been scientific racism. Through the years, scientific racism has taken many forms, all with the goal of co-opting the authority of science as objective knowledge to justify racial inequality" ("Confronting Anti-Black Racism" n.d.). An example of this is found in an article titled "Improving the Race" published in Vermont's Essex County *Herald* in 1904. It quotes Professor Francis Galton (a then well-known English biologist and eugenicist) on his purported effort to improve the human race using eugenics: "It must be introduced into the national conscience, like a new religion. It has indeed strong claims to become an orthodox religious tenet of the future, for eugenics co-operates with the workings of nature by securing that humanity shall be represented by the fittest races. What nature does blindly, slowly and ruthlessly man may do providently, quickly and kindly" ("Improving the Race" 1904).

These ideas found fertile ground among some Christian thinkers of various denominations. White supremacy discovered a temporary ally in unethical "science."

Racial supremacy and slavery renewed their vows, and by the end of the 1890s the white Southern culture implemented and became increasingly proficient at a violent system of racial terror and segregation that became known as "Jim Crow." At the core of this abhorrent system was lynching. According to Cone, "Lynching was the white community's way of forcibly reminding blacks of their inferiority and powerlessness" (Cone 2011, 7). Records maintained by the NAACP indicate that between 1882 and 1968 a total of 4,743 lynchings occurred, of which 3,446 were of Black persons (NAACP 2023). The 2015 report by the Equal Justice Initiative (EJI) of lynchings that took place between 1877 and 1950 increased that number to 4,084 Black persons lynched (Equal Justice Initiative 2017). The EJI updated its report in 2020, and that number now sits conservatively at nearly 6,500 documented lynchings that took place between 1865 and 1876, during the short-lived Reconstruction era: "Dozens of mass lynchings took place during Reconstruction in communities across the country in which hundreds of Black people were killed. Tragically, the rate of *unknown* lynchings of Black people during Reconstruction is also almost certainly dramatically higher than the thousands of unknown lynchings that took place between 1877 and 1950, for which no documentation can be found. The retaliatory killings of Black people by white Southerners immediately following the Civil War alone likely number in the thousands" (Equal Justice Initiative 2020).

While the multigenerational plight of enslaved and oppressed Black people in the United States is unparalleled, other groups also suffered under the terror of this system. In 1891, eleven Italian immigrants were lynched in New Orleans. An official apology was issued to Italian Americans on April 12, 2019, by mayor of New Orleans LaToya Cantrell (Flynn 2019). Twenty years before those lynchings, on October 24, 1871, a mass lynching of eighteen Chinese immigrants took place in Los Angeles (Zesch 2012, 178, 220). Scott Zesch in his book *The China-town War: Chinese Los Angeles and the Massacre of 1871* reported the then commonly held opinion by whites that "Chinese were 'a race marked as inferior.' Therefore, it was critical to shield white people from their influence" (2012, 194). According to the eyewitness report in the articles published at the time, these public lynchings were "enjoyed" and met with "applause," and "cheers" by the persons who participated and gathered for the incident. These acts of violence displayed a blatant disregard for the law and the dignity of fellow human be-ings—a dignity that the Bible reveals is granted by God. If we are all made to bear the image of our Creator, as Genesis 1:27 (NKJV) indicates,[7] then it is rea-sonable that God would demand that an impartial process of justice be an essential part of respecting that fundamental identity (Deut.16:18–20 NIV).[8] Therefore, the pain and injustice inflicted on any of God's image bearers, large in mass or smaller in number, equally breaks the heart of God.

Despite immense persecution, Black-led churches and denominations flour-ished. In 1890, according to a Pew Research Center article titled "A Brief Overview of Black Religious History in the US," "The US Census Bureau count-ed nearly 2.7 million 'negro communicants' at Christian churches . . . at least a fourfold increase in black Christians over the previous three decades" (Mohamed et al., 2021). To the amazement of many, something happened among the African American population when the Christ of Christianity became increasingly real and accessible to them. I submit to you that this belief in the Gospel of Jesus Christ, and its Old Testament foundation, is at the heart of what emboldened countless Black citizens, preachers, parishioners, and abolitionists to fight for liberty and justice in this new land they called home.

In the midst of their Christian experiences and citizenship (post–Fourteenth Amendment), Africans in the United States experienced a new crisis of identity. A history that included being sold into slavery by people who looked like them and who were from their places of origin—from which they were now cut off—forced them to raise their children in the New World by forging a hybrid identity. This identity, in part, honored their Blackness and some semblance of their cultural heritage, but it also sought to understand who they could be so as to survive—and for some, thrive—in their new reality. They could not simply depend on African countries for help; therefore, this new hybrid identity needed to be grounded in the hope that the future could be different—better—for Black people in the United States. W. E. B. Du Bois (2014) made a profound statement in his book *The Souls of Black Folk* that introduced his concept of "double-consciousness," which I find illustrates the tension of the hybrid identity I mention here. Speaking of the American Negro, as he puts it, Du Bois asserted:

> He would not Africanize America, for America has too much to teach the world and Africa. He would not bleach his Negro soul in a flood of white Americanism, for he knows that Negro blood has a message for the world. He simply wishes to make it possible for a man to be both Negro and American, without being cursed and spit upon by his fellows, without having the doors of Opportunity closed roughly in his face. (2014, 5)

This hope for a better future was nurtured in large part through the growth of the African American religious community. Sernett, affirming the importance of the religious community for African Americans, wrote, "Religious belonging is an elemental bond of group identity. Communities define themselves around a set of religious beliefs, symbols, and rituals. . . . [M]ost African Americans have adopted and adapted Christian, chiefly Protestant, traditions to mark their place on the pluralistic American landscape" (Sernett 1999, 3).

As Black people fought for their own liberation, the Black church became their place of prayer, power, and planning. "The more black people struggled against white supremacy, the more they found in the cross [of Christ] the spiritual power to resist the violence they so often suffered" (Cone 2011, 22). This social and spiritual journey is evidence that God heard the cries, saw the plight of oppressed African Americans, and remembered His covenant with Abraham that "All peoples on earth will be blessed through you" (Genesis 12:3b New International Version [NIV] of the Bible). And like the fulfillment of this promise to the people of Israel (who were at that time enslaved in Egypt), as recorded in Exodus

2:25 (NKJV)—"God looked upon the children of Israel, and God acknowledged them"—so too, God looked upon the oppressed children of Africa, and God acknowledged them.

This acknowledgment by God addressed the same "Christianity of this land" church—the one that could not fight against racial oppression because it was divided on its spiritual and ethical legitimacy—to "let my people go." Consequently, it was also the same Gospel of the Christian faith that convicted hearts and minds and chastised the racist practices of applicable denominational bodies within the church at large. According to the Bible, it is God's intention for His ethnically and culturally diverse creation to progress toward a more equitable and harmonious coexistence.[9] This begins with the awareness and acknowledgment that we are a nation of neighbors, who are instructed to "treat people the same way you want them to treat you" (Luke 6:31 New American Standard Bible [NASB]). The churches that failed to embody this virtue could not at the same time please God and mistreat African Americans. This haunting atrocity demanded a reckoning and a sincere repentance of past and current sins—in this case, the crimes of slavery, racism, and oppression. The church's role in propagating and practicing these crimes necessitated that such reckoning and repentance be public and institutional, as whole denominations were polluted with both historical and recurring instances of these ills. Most notable of the three mentioned here is the Southern Baptist Convention (SBC), founded in 1845 on the right to maintain slaves. Ninety-two years after its founding, the following statement was included in a "Resolution on Lynching and Mob Violence," at the SBC Annual Meeting held in New Orleans, May 13–16, 1937: "That we shall not be satisfied or content until lynchings shall cease and mob violence shall be completely banished." In 1995, the SBC acknowledged and repented of the sin of its founding and the ensuing racism practiced by members within its convention of churches over its then 150-year history.[10]

In 2000 the United Methodist Church held a service of repentance over the sin of racism and "lingering racism" in its churches.[11] In 2022 the Presbyterian Church (USA) acknowledged and repented of the sin of racism and its complicity with slavery and segregation practices. Other religious bodies have in similar fashion made public statements of apology at various times throughout their institutional history. For example: In 1985 Pope John Paul II, on behalf of the Catholic Church, issued an apology to Africans for the Catholic Church's involvement in slavery and the slave trade (Dionne 1985, 3).[12] As denominational institutions renounced and repented of their past complicity with slavery and with perpetuating racist ideologies and practices, they availed themselves of opportunities to come clean and engage in meaningful racial reconciliation efforts.

## TOWARD LIBERATION

Advocating for equal rights and fair treatment was already central to the social and spiritual mission of the Black church. Many white allies participated in that struggle going back to the 1800s—some religious, some social, some political, some literary. This modeled the premise that movements addressing national levels of social change require diverse populations of the church and society at large working collaboratively to that end. The Civil Rights Act of 1964, the Voting Rights Act of 1965, and the Fair Housing Act of 1968 were passed to ensure that the Fourteenth and Fifteenth Amendments were fairly applied to all persons and in particular to persons of color. This could not happen without the Black church, and the church could not do it by sheer institutional influence alone. This is a responsibility for all people—Black people, white people, and every hue in between, men, women, the rich, the poor, the historically oppressed, and those who were oppressors, the religious, and the nonreligious, elected officials and citizens.[13] The Earth being "full of the Lord's unfailing love" extends grace to humanity in ways that are unifying but also sometimes vexing. Vexing because, to the oppressed, the oppressor deserves no grace; and to the oppressor, the oppressed is not worthy of consideration for grace. However, I submit that it is only when we see our true condition, personally and historically, from God's perspective, that we better understand the necessity of grace and the responsible application of justice. This is the legacy of the cross of Christ where love and justice collided. It was horrible and holy, painful and pure, righteous and redemptive. To neglect this legacy of Christ in the pursuit of freedom, justice, and political reform is to exclude the very One Who dismantles principalities and powers hidden in systems and hearts, and Who persuades lawmakers to lean into His paths of justice.

It is important to note that the legacy of the cross of Christ and its Old Testament foundation has raised significant concerns for some scholars and has not been received as liberating in all contexts, which Cone pointed out in his preface to the 1997 edition of his book *God of the Oppressed* (xii). For example: The previously mentioned process of liberation of the children of Israel not only necessitated the plagues of Egypt and the demise of the Egyptian oppressors that pursued them, but their liberation also led them to an already occupied territory to displace its occupants and claim that land as their "Promised Land," granted to them by God. Their possession of that Promised Land included a massive loss of civilian life among the inhabitants that should not be overlooked or minimized. Consequently, the liberation parallels drawn from these Old Testament passages for the enslaved and formerly enslaved Black person may not have accounted for the other lenses through which such passages could be interpreted in different contexts or lived experiences. The rhetoric of "getting to the Promised Land" in Black preaching often referred to a future hope of socioeconomic equality and equity in justice, education, housing, and employment, and sometimes heaven. The primary lens was Black enslavement and oppression seeking liberation. Cone explained how different "social existences" shape our experience and eventually our theology: "Unlike Europeans who immigrated to this land to escape from tyranny, Africans came in chains to serve a nation of tyrants. It was the slave experience that shaped our idea of this land. And this difference in social existence between Europeans and Africans must be recognized, if we are to understand correctly the contrast in the form and content of black and white theology" (Cone 1997, 49).

Therefore, different theological traditions can rightfully read and critique the interpretation of the same narratives differently. Cone goes on to further explain that "the form of black religious thought is expressed in the style of story and its content is liberation" (49). So, while "whites debated the validity of infant baptism or the issue of predestination and free will; blacks recited biblical stories about God leading the Israelites from Egyptian bondage, Joshua and the battle of Jericho, and the Hebrew children in the fiery furnace" (49). The liberating God of these stories acts on behalf of the oppressed and "will break in pieces the oppressor" (Psalm 72:4b NKJV) and will "punish the world for its evil" (Isaiah 13:11a NKJV).

Looking to God as liberator does require that one reside in the context of the oppressed as an oppressed person—it is not vicarious. It is from this position that one better understands the application of various biblical texts as a liberating force. Cone asserted, "Liberation is not a human possession but a divine gift of freedom to those who struggle in faith against violence and oppression. Liberation is not an object but the project of freedom wherein the oppressed realize that their fight for freedom is a divine right of creation" (Cone 1997, 127). Understanding liberation from the perspective of chattel slavery is different than understanding it from the viewpoint of slavery to a sin condition. The latter is more descriptive of slaveholders, who were also enslaved, in that sense, to their sins and their false ideology of supremacy. Theirs was a psychological bondage and ethical deficiency that facilitated a specific type of social evil—the sins and crimes of an immoral disposition (trafficking, murder, rape, racism, injustice, cheating, etc.), as Frederick Douglass described. Of this Jesus said, "Whoever commits sin is a slave of sin" (John 8:34b NKJV). While this was a different kind of bondage, it nonetheless presented a need for liberation. The cross of Christ emerges as the leading historical and spiritual location where both the oppressed and the oppressor can go to be liberated. While the same Jesus can be seen and encountered from different perspectives by the oppressed and the oppressor, there is one posture that enables us all to see Jesus as a redemptive liberator, and that is a posture of repentance and personal humility at the cross of Christ. The biblical text asserts that His death was for our forgiveness, and His resurrection was for our transformation—now and hereafter.[14]

Cone, writing on the cross of Christ and lynching, stated, "He [Jesus] was crucified by the same principalities and powers that lynched black people in America. Because God was present with Jesus on the cross and thereby refused to let Satan and death have the last word about his meaning, God was also present at every lynching in the United States" (Cone 2011, 158). Theologically speaking, Cone seems to identify a human and a metaphysical reality at work at the cross of Christ and in the lynching experience. I would argue that this is the prevailing historical reality of the human predicament—that principalities and powers are constantly at work through systems, political dispensations, and people.[15] Some of these forces can motivate the worst in humanity, to which people can choose to either acquiesce or resist. Moving toward liberation would demand that both the human and the spiritual, in this case principalities and powers that motivate human systems, be addressed. Liberation cannot be fully actualized until both the oppressed and oppressors are free. They are bound in their respective condition together but in different positions of power at different periods in history.

Herein lies the tension and my hypothesis. Movements are stronger, more effective, and have a longer lasting impact when prayer, which engages God, and protest, which engages the systems and structures, work hand in hand. Without both we cannot effectively address the spiritual or metaphysical aspects of the human predicament. Without both it leads to results that are short lived and that eventually reveal the flaws of the strategy and the corruptible virtues and vulnerabilities of those who lead it. Cone's insightful observation that "Europeans immigrated here to escape tyranny" only to become tyrants is indicative of the human proclivity that the oppressed can themselves become oppressors. Liberation is a long journey because God is often after both the enslaved and the enslaver, the oppressed and the oppressor, through sustainable methods implemented within their societal and political context, alongside an authentic spiritually fortified church, which is necessary to resist negative spiritual influences (principalities and powers, Satan, as Cone points out). However, when the religious community is a part of the problem, and not a part of the solution, societal evils are amplified. "Upright citizens are good for a city and make it prosper, but the talk of the wicked tears it apart" (Proverbs 11:11 New Living Translation [NLT]).

## TOWARD COMMON GROUND

Righteousness and justice are the foundation of God's approach to the human condition. When we move toward justice, we ought not to neglect righteousness; and when we move toward righteousness, we ought not to neglect justice. They are inseparable—you cannot truly have one without the other. When we pursue both, through prayer, protest, and eventually policy, we cooperate with God. When we do not, we create social and political systems that eventually lead to periodic and even chronic failures of the systems and increase the likelihood of long-term dysfunction in our social constructs. God's inclusion can, however, provide a shared understanding of personhood and purpose that endures the test of time and supplies the power to challenge forces—spiritual and human—that are intent on unethically or immorally subjugating people even if it is legal to do so at that point in history, as it was prior to 1863. In the book *The Black Christian Experience*, compiled by Emmanuel L. McCall in 1972, Otis Moss Jr. in his chapter on "Black Church Distinctives" wrote what I consider a description of God's activity in our pain, pursuits, and prayers: "The Black church has converted oppression into poetry, exploitation into creative force, humiliation into a hunger for justice, haunting fears into hymns of faith. If this church is to remain relevant, it must convert a praying people into a positive power-conscious people. Prayer must find fulfillment in revolutionary action. Remember that prayer without action is empty. Remember also that action without prayer is dangerous" (McCall 1972, 15–16).

Prayer, protest, and policy must still work together. Prayer invites God into our problems, protests, and plans.

Christian Smith, professor of sociology at the University of Notre Dame, pointed out in the introduction to his edited book *Disruptive Religion: The Force of Faith in Social Movement Activism* that "Religion can help to keep everything in its place. But it can also turn the world upside-down" (Smith 1996, 1). This resonates because it was also said of the early church in Acts 17:6 (NKJV): "But when they did not find them, they dragged Jason and some brethren to the rulers of the city, crying out, 'These who have turned the world upside down have come here too.'" Smith further argues that "it is clear that religion has often played, and today still plays, an absolutely central role in a number of important social and political movements. Indeed, in a host of cases, religion has served as the primary source of many of the necessary ingredients of social-movement emergence and success" (1). While much has changed in society since Smith published this work, and while religious extremism (regardless of faith tradition) and/or secular extremism have proven to only harm society, I still contend that without a balanced authentic religious influence, the desire to genuinely see each other beyond racial stereotypes will remain a lingering challenge. Viewing others as neighbors is critical to understanding the influence Jesus had and still has on the world and the kind of community the church is intended to become.[16] Any extreme version of biblical/religious teaching that morphs into a bigoted oppressive ideology is not "Christianity proper," just as Frederick Douglass rightfully determined about slaveholders' "Christianity of this land."

The answer would not be to seek to rid society of religious influence, nor to ignore it, but instead to ensure that our praxis is connected to God and the people and not only to causes. According to the Gospel writers, Jesus encountered religious leaders who lacked a real and vital connection with God and because of that did not really serve the people. They only served their own prosperity. Of them, the Scripture said, "These people honor me [God] with their lips, but their hearts are far from me [God]. Their worship is a farce, for they teach man-made ideas as commands from God" (Matt. 15:8–9 NLT). The further our hearts move away from God and from the people we serve, the less effective our efforts seem to become. The sociopolitical influence of the Black church and Black organizations influenced by the Black church community is well documented through the civil rights movement. Black people in the United States are a testament to the value of the connected religious community in creating and motivating change within its social context. However, none of this was/is possible without the resourceful and sustaining work of God's grace and the empowerment of God's Spirit in the hearts and minds of a people determined to be liberated. Henry Louis Gates Jr. in his latest book, *The Black Church: This Is Our Story, This Is Our Song*, captured this well: "The miracle of African American survival can be traced directly to the miraculous ways that our ancestors—across a range of denominations and through the widest variety of worship—reinvented the religion that their 'masters' thought would keep them subservient. Rather, that religion enabled them and their descendants to learn, to grow, to develop, to interpret and reinvent the world in which they were trapped" (Gates 2021, xxiii).

I view Gates's use of the term *reinvent* as effectively speaking of God's redemptive activity, through "Christianity proper," enabling and emboldening African Americans to lift themselves from the lies of racial inferiority and reinvent their learned understanding of themselves—what Carter G. Woodson called their "mis-education" (2010)—and emerge from their sufferings with the spiritual fortitude to continue reinventing the world within themselves and simultaneously the world around them. Unlearning false ideologies and false constructs is a part of liberation.

The Black church community and movements of today—that continue to explore liberative paradigms, theories, and theologies—whose roots historically were once linked, must be aware of the temptation to exclude or substitute God for causes alone. Perhaps progress has a side effect that, if we are not careful, can diminish our capacity to appreciate the necessity of God in motivating progress. Thus, success in our causes can become a "god" that propels us onto paths that are no longer connected to righteousness and justice but are connected to affluence, pride, and just us. Such a warning was issued in Deuteronomy 8:11–14,18a (NLT):

> But that is the time to be careful! Beware that in your plenty you do not forget the Lord your God and disobey his commands, regulations, and decrees that I am giving you today. [12] For when you have become full and prosperous and have built fine homes to live in, [13] and when your flocks and herds have become very large and your silver and gold have multiplied along with everything else, be careful! [14] Do not become proud at that time and forget the Lord your God, who rescued you from slavery in the land of Egypt. . . . [18] Remember the Lord your God. He is the one who gives you power to be successful.

When we forget, we can form and practice new types of segregation—a segregation of the heart—from God and from "others." In his book *Strength to Love*, Martin Luther King Jr., expounding on the "Man Who Was a Fool," wrote, "Jesus called the rich man a fool because he failed to realize his dependence on God. He talked as though he unfolded the seasons and provided the fertility of the soil, controlled the rising and setting of the sun, and regulated the natural processes that produced the rain and the dew. He had an unconscious feeling that he was the Creator, not a creature" (King 1963a, 69).

He also wrote, "The rich man was a fool because he failed to realize his dependence on others. His soliloquy contains approximately sixty words, yet 'I' and 'my' occur twelve times. He has said 'I' and 'my' so often that he had lost the capacity to say 'we' and 'our'" (69). King's interpretation of the text highlights the necessity of both the vertical (with God) and the horizontal (with others) relationships. We need each other, and oftentimes it is only the common ground of our pain that humbles us to see that. Therefore, I propose that finding and maintaining common ground necessitates three things: 1. remembering our pain in constructive ways, and/or processing the pain from the pain one caused, in constructive ways; 2. depending on God; and 3. collaborating with others.

First, how do we find common ground? By creating spaces for conversations, lectures, documentaries, and films as tools to listen to each other tell our stories and read our stories. Not comparing them in terms of whose pain was more traumatic, or whose privilege carried them quicker toward justice; but listening first to historical experiences and their impact and allowing it to give us a glimpse into each other's soul. This constructive glimpse should be grounded in facts and feelings, yet its frequency and technique should be managed so as to strike a healthy balance between overload and forgetfulness.

Second, how do we live on common ground? By respecting God enough to respect each other as equals. It is imperative that we operate with the knowledge that we do not confer value or equality unto others; it is inherent because of *imago Dei*—we all have the image of God. Therefore, we can only recognize and honor this, as should our laws. This recognition must not be mere sentiment but be codified into law in a way that reminds and reprimands. Laws and public policies become the neutral ground upon which all in society could have equal rights, including the right to peacefully disagree and protest, while carefully avoiding the pitfalls of religious extremism and/or secular domination. It is equally important that an individual does not see him- or herself as inferior to other persons. Both the law and the church are needed to create and maintain a healthy tension between an exclusively secular approach and religious participation in the pursuit of living righteously and justly on common ground.

Third, how do we thrive on common ground? By collaborating in ways that eliminate the artificial social barriers that limit mobility and success, and elevating a mindset that contributes to growth, excellence, and the good of all in a society. Such elevation is multilayered and multigenerational. It must facilitate access to opportunities while maintaining the standard of the opportunity and at the same time level the field sufficiently to ensure that environmental and educational spaces, especially for the youngest among us, adequately prepare people to understand, inform, and meet those equitable standards so that they may gain access to these opportunities and eventually to shared power. Therefore, if we are to continue on a path toward equity and understanding, we must do it together. The Rev. Dr. Martin Luther King Jr., in his 1963 "I Have a Dream" speech, said these words, which continue to speak volumes to the church and society: "The marvelous new militancy which has engulfed the Negro community must not lead us to a distrust of all white people, for many of our white brothers, as evidenced by their presence here today, have come to realize that their destiny is tied up with our destiny. And they have come to realize that their freedom is inextricably bound to our freedom" (King 1963b). In a similar vein, Cone, presenting his final analysis concerning our predicament, wrote:

> Blacks and whites are bound together in Christ by their brutal and beautiful encounter in this land. Neither blacks or whites can be understood fully without reference to the other because of their common religious heritage as well as their joint relationship to the lynching experience. What happened to blacks also happened to whites. When whites lynched blacks, they were literally and symbolically lynching themselves—their sons, daughters, cousins, mothers and fathers, and a host of other relatives. Whites may be bad brothers and sisters, murderers of their own black kin, but they are still our sisters and brothers. We are bound together in America by faith and tragedy. All the hatred we have expressed toward one another cannot destroy the profound mutual love and solidarity that flow deeply between us—a love that empowered blacks to open their arms to receive the many whites who were also empowered by the same love to risk their lives in the black struggle for freedom. (Cone 2011, 165–166)

## CONCLUSION

God has liberated, is liberating, and will liberate humanity—"the earth is full of His unfailing love." May we continue to learn to listen to each other and love righteousness and justice, which are "the foundation of God's throne." We have a way of memorializing our struggles and our life lessons into songs. It is a means by which we remind ourselves and inform future generations of the journey of our people. I find such relevant and deeply moving content in the Black National Anthem, "Lift Every Voice and Sing," written by James Weldon Johnson and set to music by his composer brother, John Rosamond Johnson (1921). In it I hear a people learning to rejoice yet knowing that the fight for freedom remains ever before them. Do you hear it? In it I hear the weariness of a long and arduous journey to a present reality that speaks of a brighter future. Do you hear it? In it I hear the caution of a people to remain connected to God as they progress and not become so intoxicated with the "wine of the world" (perhaps starter-liberties that can influence one to trade ongoing progress for distracting pleasures, temporary prosperity, or fleeting popularity) that we stray from the God who is liberating us. Do you hear it? In it I hear forgiveness—through the embracing of a native land from which Black bodies were captured and also sold, and a land that is now called home (native), where Black bodies were abused. To be true to this/these land(s) required forgiveness. Do you hear it?

I pray that we can enter into the spirit of this song and its meaning for those whose paths have intersected with the pain of oppression and the joy of liberation.

## LIFT EVERY VOICE AND SING

Lift every voice and sing
Till earth and heaven ring,
Ring with the harmonies of Liberty;
Let our rejoicing rise
High as the listening skies,
Let it resound loud as the rolling sea.
Sing a song full of the faith that the dark past has taught us,
Sing a song full of the hope that the present has brought us,
Facing the rising sun of our new day begun
Let us march on till victory is won.

Stony the road we trod,
Bitter the chastening rod,
Felt in the days when hope unborn had died;
Yet with a steady beat,
Have not our weary feet
Come to the place for which our fathers sighed?
We have come over a way that with tears have been watered,
We have come, treading our path through the blood of the slaughtered,
Out from the gloomy past,
Till now we stand at last
Where the white gleam of our bright star is cast.

God of our weary years,
God of our silent tears,
Thou who hast brought us thus far on the way;
Thou who hast by Thy might led us into the light,
Keep us forever in the path, we pray.
Lest our feet stray from the places, our God, where we met Thee.
Lest our hearts, drunk with the wine of the world, we forget Thee;

Shadowed beneath Thy hand, may we forever stand,
True to our God,
True to our native land.

## Notes

[1] Taken from Acts 8:26–38 (NKJV). [26] "Now an angel of the Lord spoke to Philip, saying, 'Arise and go toward the south along the road which goes down from Jerusalem to Gaza.' This is desert. [27] So he arose and went. And behold, a man of Ethiopia, a eunuch of great authority under Candace the queen of the Ethiopians, who had charge of all her treasury, and had come to Jerusalem to worship, [28] was returning. And sitting in his chariot, he was reading Isaiah the prophet. [29] Then the Spirit said to Philip, 'Go near and overtake this chariot.' [30] So Philip ran to him, and heard him reading the prophet Isaiah, and said, 'Do you understand what you are reading?' [31] And he said, 'How can I, unless someone guides me?' [35] Then Philip opened his mouth, and beginning at this Scripture, preached Jesus to him. [36] Now as they went down the road, they came to some water. And the eunuch said, 'See, *here is* water. What hinders me from being baptized?' [37] Then Philip said, 'If you believe with all your heart, you may.' And he answered and said, 'I believe that Jesus Christ is the Son of God.' [38] So he commanded the chariot to stand still. And both Philip and the eunuch went down into the water, and he baptized him."

[2] Matt. 28:18–20 (NKJV). "And Jesus came and spoke to them, saying, 'All authority has been given to Me in heaven and on earth. [19] Go therefore and make disciples of all the nations, baptizing them in the name of the Father and of the Son and of the Holy Spirit, [20] teaching them to observe all things that I have commanded you; and lo, I am with you always, *even* to the end of the age.' Amen."

[3] Jupiter Hammon lived in the northeast between 1711 and 1806, dying just before the British ended the slave trade in 1807. In 2013, University of Texas at Arlington professor Cedrick May discovered an unpublished poem in the Yale archives that he later proved was written by Jupiter Hammon. For the article on May's discovery, see *Yale Alumni Magazine* May/June 2013 at https://yalealumnimagazine.org/articles/3662-an-enslaved-poet-on-slavery," which suggests that his latter position on slavery was not best reflected in his earlier published works, and that he was more outspoken against slavery than previously determined (May and McCown 2013).

[4] Douglass lived from 1818 to 1895 and experienced life before the Civil War, life during Reconstruction, and saw the start of the Jim Crow era.

[5] The issuance of the proclamation of the end of the American Civil War was on August 20, 1866, by President Andrew Johnson.

[6] The Reconstruction era saw the passing of several amendments and acts to protect the rights of freed Black citizens. For access to Reconstruction era laws and documents, see ProQuest. Part of Clarivate (n.d.)

[7] Gen. 1:27 states, [27] "So God created man in His *own* image; in the image of God He created him; male and female He created them."

[8] Deut. 16:18–20 states, [18] "Appoint judges and officials for yourselves from each of your tribes in all the towns the Lord your God is giving you. They must judge the people fairly. [19] You must never twist justice or show partiality. Never accept a bribe, for bribes blind the eyes of the wise and corrupt the decisions of the godly. [20] Let true justice prevail, so you may live and occupy the land that the Lord your God is giving you."

[9] According to Galatians all nations regardless of culture or historical beliefs have access to God through faith in Jesus Christ—a faith that then dismantles the artificial walls of separation between humanity, be it nationality, social status, or gender. Gal. 3:26–29 states, [26] "For you are all sons of God through faith in Christ Jesus. [27] For as many of you as were baptized into Christ have put on Christ. [28] There is neither Jew nor Greek, there is neither slave nor free, there is neither male nor female; for you are all one in Christ Jesus. [29] And if you *are* Christ's, then you are Abraham's seed, and heirs according to the promise."

[10] "Be it further RESOLVED, That we apologize to all African-Americans for condoning and/or perpetuating individual and systemic racism in our lifetime; and we genuinely repent of racism of which we have been guilty, whether consciously (Psalm 19:13) or unconsciously (Leviticus 4:27); and Be it further RESOLVED, That we ask forgiveness from our African-American brothers and sisters, acknowledging that our own healing is at stake; and Be it further RESOLVED, That we hereby commit ourselves to eradicate racism in all its forms from Southern Baptist life and ministry." It is important to note that the SBC, founded on the right to maintain slaves, previously made resolutions addressing matters of race relations, decrying lynching, and encouraging ethnic involvement as far back as 1937 (mentioned above) and 1939.

[11] "As white Christians we repent of our complicity in the belief in white supremacy: the belief that people of European descent are superior in intelligence, skills, imagination, and perseverance. We acknowledge that this belief in white supremacy has been the foundation of, and an excuse for, atrocities against people of African descent in the United States and in the world. We repent of our failure to recognize and take responsibility for the legacy of slavery."

[12] This was not the Catholic Church's first statement of acknowledgment concerning the ills of slavery.

[13] In the Bible we see that God works in human society through systems of governmental leadership. We also see God's judgment on systems of governmental leadership when they consistently fail to administer justice, or when they consistently function corruptly. Romans 13:1–7 speaks to the former. Nahum 3:1–19 speaks to the latter.

[14] This text refers prophetically to Jesus's death on the cross. Isaiah 53:5, "But he [Jesus] was pierced for our transgressions, he was crushed for our iniquities; the punishment that brought us peace was on him, and by his wounds we are healed." 1 Peter 1:3–4, "Praise be to the God and Father of our Lord Jesus Christ! In his great mercy he has given us new birth into a living hope through the resurrection of Jesus Christ from the dead, and into an inheritance that can never perish, spoil or fade. This inheritance is kept in heaven for you."

[15] Walter Wink deals extensively with this idea of how metaphysical forces identified broadly as principalities and powers manifest in human societies, systems, and situations. See his trilogy: *Naming the Powers: The Language of Power in the New Testament* (1984); *Unmasking the Powers: The Invisible Powers That Determine Human Existence* (1986); and *Engaging the Powers: Discernment and Resistance in a World of Domination* (1992).

[16] Matthew 22:37–40 teaches this principle, that everything hangs on learning to love God and others. It states, "Jesus replied: 'Love the Lord your God with all your heart and with all your soul and with all your mind.' [38] This is the first and greatest commandment. [39] And the second is like it: 'Love your neighbor as yourself.' [40] All the Law and the Prophets hang on these two commandments."

## Works Cited

Allen, Richard. 1960. *The Life Experience and Gospel Labors of the Rt. Rev. Richard Allen*. Nashville: Abingdon Press.

Barnes, Albert. 1857. *The Church and Slavery*. Philadelphia: Parry & McMillan. Reprinted 1969 by Negro Universities Press: A Division of Greenwood Press, New York.

Cone, James H. 1997. *God of the Oppressed* (New Rev. Ed.). Maryknoll, NY: Orbis Books.

Cone, James H. 2011. *The Cross and the Lynching Tree*. Maryknoll, NY: Orbis Books.

"Confronting Anti-Black Racism: Scientific Racism." n.d. Harvard Library. https://library.harvard.edu/confronting-anti-black-racism/scientific-racism. Accessed July 4, 2023.

Dionne, Jr., E. J. 1985. "Pope Apologizes to Africans for Slavery." *New York Times*, August 14, Section A, 3. https://www.nytimes.com/1985/08/14/world/pope-apologizes-to-africans-for-slavery.html.

Douglass, Frederick. 1849. *Narrative of the Life of Frederick Douglass, an American Slave*. Boston: The Anti-Slavery Office. Library of Congress. https://www.loc.gov/resource/lhbcb.25385/?sp=3&st=image.

Du Bois, W. E. B. 2014. *The Souls of Black Folk*. North Haven, CT: Millennium Publications. Originally published in 1903 in Chicago by A. C. McClurg and Co.

Equal Justice Initiative. 2017. "Lynching in America: Confronting the Legacy of Racial Terror" (3rd Ed.). https://eji.org/reports/lynching-in-america/.

Equal Justice Initiative. 2020. "Reconstruction in America: Racial Violence after the Civil War, 1865–1876." https://eji.org/reports/reconstruction-in-america-overview/.

Flynn, Meagan. 2019. "New Orleans to Apologize for Lynching of 11 Italians in 1891, among Worst in American History." *The Washington Post*, April 1. https://www.washingtonpost.com/nation/2019/04/01/new-orleans-apologize-lynching-italians-among-worst-american-history/.

Franklin, John Hope and Alfred A. Moss, Jr. 1988. *From Slavery to Freedom: A History of Negro Americans* (6th Ed.). New York: McGraw-Hill.

Gates, Jr., Henry Louis. 2021. *The Black Church: This Is Our Story, This Is Our Song.* New York: Penguin Press. Kindle Edition.

Gerbner, Katharine. 2018. *Christian Slavery: Conversion and Race in the Protestant Atlantic World.* Philadelphia, PA: University of Pennsylvania Press. Kindle Edition.

Harvey, Paul. 1997. *Redeeming the South: Religious Cultures and Racial Identities Among Southern Baptists 1865–1925.* Chapel Hill: University of North Carolina Press.

Hochschild, Adam. 2005. *Bury the Chains: Prophets and Rebels in the Fight to Free an Empire's Slaves.* New York: Houghton Mifflin Harcourt. Kindle Edition.

"Improving the Race." 1904. *Essex County Herald*, 1873–1964, Vol. XXXII, August 5, Guildhall, VT. https://chroniclingamerica.loc.gov/data/batches/vtu_ira_ver01/data/sn84023416/00202197541/1904080501/0778.pdf.

Johnson, James Weldon (set to music by John Rosamond Johnson). "Lift Every Voice and Sing." New York: E. B. Marks Music Co, 1921. Notated music. https://www.loc.gov/item/89751755/.

Keel, Terence D. 2013. "Religion, Polygenism and the Early Science of Human Origins." *History of the Human Sciences*, Vol. 26, No. 2, 3–32. University of California Santa Barbara, USA, https://www.history.ucsb.edu/wp-content/uploads/History-of-the-Human-Sciences-2013-Keel-3-32.pdf.

King, Jr., Martin Luther. 1963a. *Strength to Love.* Minneapolis: Fortress Press.

King, Jr., Martin Luther. 1963b. "I Have a Dream." Lincoln Memorial, Washington DC, August 28. https://www.archives.gov/nyc/exhibit/mlk.

Liston, Robert. 1970. *Slavery in America: The History of Slavery.* New York: McGraw-Hill Book Company.

Lovejoy, Paul E. 2012. *Transformations in Slavery: A History of Slavery in Africa* (3rd Ed.). Cambridge: Cambridge University Press. Kindle Edition.

May, Cedrick and Julie McCown. 2013. "'An Essay on Slavery': An Unpublished Poem by Jupiter Hammon." *Early American Literature*, Vol. 48, No. 2, 457–471. University of North Carolina Press. http://www.jstor.org/stable/24476358.

McCall, Emmanuel L. (Compiler). 1972. *The Black Christian Experience.* Nashville, TN: Broadman Press.

Mohamed, Besheer, et al. 2021. "A Brief Overview of Black Religious History in the U.S." Pew Research Center. https://www.pewresearch.org/religion/2021/02/16/a-brief-overview-of-black-religious-history-in-the-u-s/.

NAACP. 2023. "History of Lynching in America." https://naacp.org/find-resources/history-explained/history-lynching-america.

Plante, Trevor K. 2015. "Ending the Bloodshed: The Last Surrenders of the Civil War." The U.S. National Archives and Records Administration. Spring, Vol. 47, No. 1. https://www.archives.gov/publications/prologue/2015/spring/cw-surrenders.html.

Presbyterian Church (USA). 2022. "On Offering an Apology to African Americans for the Sin of Slavery and Its Legacy." 225th General Assembly, Louisville, KY, June. https://www.pc-biz.org/#/search/3000895.

ProQuest: Part of Clarivate. "Civil War and Reconstruction Era (1861–1877)." https://blackfreedom.proquest.com/category/civil-war-and-reconstruction-era/.

Sernett, Milton C. 1999. *African American Religious History: A Documentary Witness* (2nd Ed.). Durham: Duke University Press.

Shannon, Sr., David T. 2012. *George Liele's Life and Legacy: An Unsung Hero*. Macon, GA: Mercer University Press.

Smith, Christian. 1996. *Disruptive Religion: The Force of Faith in Social Movement Activism*, edited by Christian Smith. New York/London: Routledge.

Southern Baptist Convention. 1937. "Resolution on Lynching and Mob Violence." New Orleans, LA, May 13–16. https://www.sbc.net/resource-library/resolutions/resolution-on-lynching-and-mob-violence/.

Southern Baptist Convention. 1995. "Resolution on Racial Reconciliation on the 150th Anniversary of the Southern Baptist Convention," Atlanta, GA, June 20–22. https://www.sbc.net/resource-library/resolutions/resolution-on-racial-reconciliation-on-the-150th-anniversary-of-the-southern-baptist-convention/.

United Methodist Church. 2000. "United Methodists Repent for Racism." United Methodist General Conference, Cleveland, OH, May 5. http://gc2000.org/gc2000news/stories/gc019.htm.

Wills, Gregory A. 2009. *Southern Baptist Theological Seminary 1859–2009*. New York: Oxford University Press.

Wink, Walter. 1984. *Naming the Powers: The Language of Power in the New Testament*. Philadelphia: Fortress Press.

Wink, Walter. 1986. *Unmasking the Powers: The Invisible Powers That Determine Human Existence*. Minneapolis: Fortress Press.

Wink, Walter. 1992. *Engaging the Powers: Discernment and Resistance in a World of Domination*. Minneapolis: Fortress Press.

Woodson, Carter Godwin. 2010. *The Mis-Education of the Negro*. Las Vegas: CreateSpace Independent Publishing Platform.

Zesch, Scott. 2012. *The Chinatown War: Chinese Los Angeles and the Massacre of 1871*. New York: Oxford University Press.

# Truth and Lies about Italian American Culture: A Response to Rev. Williams's Call

FRED L. GARDAPHÉ

This response to the Rev. Williams's keynote address is based on the impromptu remarks I made the day of the symposium, as best as I can remember them; I left my notes on the podium and didn't retrieve them, so what I've done here is reconstruct the spirit of my words that day with the help of supporting material from various writings I've done over the years on the relationship of Italian Americans and African Americans. In his address, the reverend presented a magisterial sermon that spoke to the role religion played in the liberation of African Americans and how religion has enabled them to cope with the inhumane treatment they've endured for centuries. What struck me was how similar Italian American culture can be to African American culture, and yet racism divides the two.

The difference between a religion built on acceptance of one's fate and one built on a struggle for freedom is at the center of my comments. Those Italians who were brought up on Roman Catholicism in Italy were taught to accept their fate and live with the hopes of a better life after death. Those enslaved Africans who came to Christianity were kept in place by the same thinking; and religious indoctrination would keep their rebellious behavior at bay. In both cases that didn't work for many people. Many didn't wait for the next life for the freedom to control their own lives. Even when Africans left slavery, they could not leave behind the prejudices and discrimination that became obstacles to living as free human beings; Italians ran away from their unlivable conditions to make better lives in the US. As Italians became Americans, while they may have faced prejudice and discrimination, many of them nonetheless became racists. So, the first truth I will present is that Italian Americans are indeed racists, and I am one of them. I wasn't born a racist, but I became one, and this is how it happened.

Back in the 1950s, friction escalated between the Black people who lived the working-class community of Maywood, Illinois, and residents of Melrose Park, my Italian American town, just across the railroad tracks. Maywood's train station, the next stop east from where I was raised, had been a stop on the Underground Railroad for runaway slaves, but I wouldn't know this for many years. The Chicago Northwestern tracks became a border that you would drive across, but never walk over, for racism was rampant, passing from one generation to the next in the most subtle of ways.

In those days, kids played on the streets. Parents never asked what we did outside unless we did something wrong that got back to them through the gossip grapevine. We'd wake up in the morning and mothers would toss us out as soon as they could. The only warning we'd get was, "Don't talk to strangers, and stay away from the tracks." At first we didn't know why; was it the danger of being hit by a train, or some kind of contamination if we encountered those who lived on the other side? There were lessons everywhere, on streets, alleys, tar-covered rooftops, the school grounds; but I found out early that you don't understand everything you learn. When our world outside came in touch with that world of the adults, the trouble began: Their problems made our world seem tranquil; while we were ever curious about theirs, we were comfortable only in ours. With each encounter outside the house, I grew away from what I had been taught and where I had come from. I drifted away from my moral moorings but never had a sense of where I might be heading.

Our street games included marbles, strike ball against the school wall, hide and seek, capture the flag, and kick the can. We chose sides by chanting an old counting rhyme that reinforced the racist training we underwent.

Eeny, meeny, miney mo,
Catch a n----- by the toe;
If he hollers let him go.
Eeny, meeny, miney mo,

We had no idea what the n-word meant, so none of us ever thought twice about who we might be offending by launching into that seemingly innocent ditty before we'd start our games; it was our way of entering into play, we had no idea how that simple rhyme shaped our prejudice against Black people. But as we grew older, it became more and more apparent because of the way the adults in town used it. This happened when we began to cross streets with our bicycles. Bikes were the vehicles of our freedom, and with them we began pushing our boundaries. We started by riding along the tracks on our side of town. It soon shifted to daring each other to ride across them, venturing into the Black neighborhood and often being chased out. That was the closest any of us got to Black people.

It would take me years to understand that our fear of these people had nothing to do with them or how they might hurt us, but with how we in town feared we could become like them. They were the dark thoughts in our minds. One day, after hearing a news report about a civil rights march that happened in the city, my grandfather told me, "If they ever try to march around here, I'll go up on the roof and pick them off [with a rifle] one by one as they come across the tracks." I didn't dare ask him why he felt that way, but the tone in his voice told me he was serious. I began to hope that the Black population would never try to march near our place.

The hardest part about realizing that you're a racist is that the same people who taught you how to love also taught you how to hate. I have spent my whole life trying to escape those racist origins, and here's what I did along the way to change the way I thought and lived.

Beyond the horrible accounts of police brutality that were projected daily on our television screens, we were privy only to the stories told by the adults in town about their encounters with Black people. There were no Black students in our Catholic schools, so rare was the encounter with Black youth before high school. That, for me, was 1966, and while the prep school I attended didn't have any Black students, the public high school we passed each day on the bus was where most of those who lived in Melrose first encountered Black people daily. Many were the stories of fights that occurred in that school, and after the assassination of Martin Luther King, the city and its suburbs erupted in riots that shook our sleepy town worse than the 1920 Palm Sunday tornado that destroyed our church and school and killed ten residents of our town.

I participated in some of those fights and went on to live in the shame of that mob mentality behavior that swept me along my racist path. It would take time, and individual relationships with Black co-workers, friends, and even a girl-friend, before I could begin to see just what it was I had become. As I went off to college, I began to study African American culture. and years later that study led me into Italian American studies. I was involved in the first conference of what was then called the American Italian Historical Association to focus on the soci-ocultural interactions between Black Americans and Italian Americans. This conference resulted in the publication *Shades of Black and White: Conflict and Collaboration between Two Communities*. A few years later I co-edited, with Dr. William Connell, a volume titled *Anti-Italianism: Essays on a Prejudice*, which contained essays that explore the sociohistorical significance of the effects of more than a century of overt and covert discrimination against Italian immigrants to the United States.

What I have learned from these academic experiences is that the key to stud-ying Italian American experiences requires that American studies deal with two major issues: race and class. While we have done a good job of working gender and ethnicity, and to some extent race, into the courses of study, we have fallen short in our investigations of class and especially how it intersects with race. Human values can be renewed if usable pasts are recovered and reworked to guide people away from reactionary politics based on forgotten discriminated pasts that separate and divide and toward the type of revolutionary politics that unite. A hopeful possibility for this was advanced by Patrick Gallo in his 1974 study *Ethnic Alienation: The Italian-Americans*. Gallo saw enough similarities between Italian and African Americans to suggest the creation of an alliance of, in his words, "whites and Blacks, white-collar and blue-collar workers, based on mutual need and interdependence. . . . Italian-Americans may prove to be a vital ingredient in not only forging that alliance but in serving as the cement that will hold urban centers together" (26). Gallo's idea, while never formally acted upon, was echoed in Michael Parenti's more recent call for new bases for the construction of Italian American identities.

To frame the Italian American experience within a context of struggle for social justice and economic survival is to give it a dimension that goes beyond nostalgia and sentimentality and flies in the face of the stereotypes that weigh down upon Italians. Italian Americans can only enter the struggle for social justice for all by first confronting the history and process by which they came to be granted the privileges the US has historically reserved for those who could achieve whiteness.

## WHITES ON A LEASH: ITALIAN AMERICANS AND WHITE PRIVILEGE IN THE US

For Italian Americans, "making it" came at a high price, costing us the language of our ancestors—the main means by which history is preserved and heritage passed on from one generation to the next. For a few generations we have had to publicly avoid or even hide any customs that have been depicted as quaint (but labeled as alien) in order to prove equality to those higher on the ladder of success. In this way, Italian Americans have become white, but a different kind of white from those of the dominant Anglo-Saxon culture. Italian Americans have become whites on a leash. And as long as we behaved ourselves (acted white), as long as we accepted the images of ourselves presented in the media (didn't cry defamation), and as long as we stayed within corporate and sociocultural boundaries (didn't identify with other minorities) we would be allowed to remain white. This behavior has led to Italian Americans being left out of most early discussions of multiculturalism.

In *A Different Mirror*, Ronald Takaki's (1993) revision of American history, the European immigrants and their descendants are either lumped into the falsely monolithic category of whites or else overlooked entirely. The fact is that each of these groups has its own unique history of subjugation that aligns it more closely with Takaki's oppressed minorities than with the Anglo majority. We all need to come to grips with the fact that there is great diversity and much oppression within white America. Until then, we are doomed to repeat the mistakes of the earlier histories that we are trying to correct.

For too long, the US media were all too ready to help restrict Italians' attempts to assimilate as white Americans. The vast majority of Italian Americans are law-abiding citizens, but you wouldn't know it by watching television, listening to the radio, or reading books. We have been viciously framed by the constant repetition of negative portrayals. Most histories of Mafia in America begin with the 1890 murder of the corrupt New Orleans Police Chief David Hennessey. The aftermath of his murder led to one of the largest recorded mass lynchings in this country's history. American obsession with the Mafia has overshadowed the real history of Italians in America that includes indentured servitude, lynchings, Ku Klux Klan terrorism against Italians, and strong participation in civil rights struggles. For Italian Americans, overt oppression has given way to more covert techniques of discrimination. Italians have replaced Indians and Black people as the acceptable "bad guys" in films, and this image was regularly reinforced and perpetuated through contemporary remakes of gangster films that have become the building blocks of an American cultural imagination that has ossified a stereotype and fortified the possibilities of remaining white.

This never-ending reproduction of negative stereotypes has so impoverished American minds that anything Italian is immediately connected to gangsterism and ignorance, and so Italians may protest such images without a sense of what other groups have experienced. To become American, Italians would have to do everything in their power to show they were unlike the gangsters and buffoons who dominated public representation of their culture. To stay Americans, we would have to avoid anything that might make us seem in need of institutional protection of the kind granted to other minority groups.

There are many examples of Italian Americans who have both broken the silence and created the historical narratives that will challenge long-established notions of ethnic whiteness. In his keynote address to the 1994 American Italian Historical Association's national conference, Rudolph Vecoli (1996) challenged the notion of Italian Americans being white. "Our experience has taught the fallacy of the very idea of race and the mischief of racial labels. It has taught us that both total assimilation and total separatism are will-o'-the-wisps, unachievable—and undesirable if they were. It has taught us that a healthy ethnicity is compatible with, indeed essential to, a healthy America. For these reasons, we, Italian Americans, have something important to contribute to the national dialogue" (17).

Vecoli concludes his speech with the idea that the key to Italian American participation is the creation of the ability to define ourselves as "distinguished by our unique experience" that is not "white, nor black, nor brown, nor red, nor yellow" (17).

Although racial discrimination against Italians was more prevalent in the past, it has not disappeared. Today Italian American youth suffer from association with a different stereotype; the image of the organ-grinding immigrant has been replaced by the mafioso and the dumb street kid à la Rocky Balboa. These images do not come from family interaction, but from the larger society, so that when Italian Americans look into the cultural mirror, they receive a distorted view, like a fun-house mirror in an amusement park. Consciously or unconsciously those distorted images affect their identity, and they must face the reality that the dominant culture is comfortable with Italians as serio/comic figures, caricatures made up of the most distorted aspects of their culture. The question all Italian Americans must confront these days is, "Who controls the image-making process and why are their social images so distorted?" Reinforcement of a positive cultural identity that was created in the home is necessary for the maintenance of—and a willingness to continue—that identification outside the home. If children get the idea that to be Italian is to be what the media and white histories say Italian is, then they will either avoid it if it shames them or embrace it if it gets them attention.

Italians have certainly complicated the notion of whiteness in America so that they are not totally white, and it is this in-between status that makes them likely candidates to support the abolition of whiteness as a privilege status in the US. The work of scholars such as Olga Peragallo, Rose Basile Green, and Helen Barolini has enabled us to pay attention to Italian American literature, something I could not even have imagined during my earlier education. For me, American literature was not something connected to my working-class, ethnic upbringing. In college, I studied African American culture with Finley Campbell (at the University of Wisconsin, Madison), who first inspired me to begin my search for Italian American writers when he said, "White people got roots too!" Later, when I asked another professor if he thought we could study Italian American writers the way we were beginning to study African American, Latinx American, Asian American, and other groups, he responded with a laugh and something like, "No. They are white." We may have been white in his eyes, but our work certainly wasn't "white" enough to be included in his courses. This series of events pushed me forward in my search for Italian American literature and to join the work of other young scholars (at the time) Mary Jo Bona, Anthony Julian Tamburri, and Paolo Giordano, who through our own inherent version of indigenousness were looking for the knowledge of our ancestors. This work required finding the nearly invisible people called Italian American.

## INVISIBILITY AND THE ITALIAN AMERICAN

> "I am invisible, understand, simply because people refuse to see me."
> —Ralph Ellison

Italian Americans are invisible people. Not, because people refuse to see them, but because, for the most part, they refuse to be seen. Italian Americans became invisible the moment they could pass as white. And since then, they have gone to great extremes to avoid being identified as anything but white. They have even hidden the history of being people of color.

Whether they like it or not, Italian Americans cannot escape the fact that they weren't always white. They were lynched, burned out of homes, chased, captured, and killed by the Ku Klux Klan. At the direction of politicians and businessmen they were herded into ghettos and then redlined into acceptable areas after ghetto relocation. They were discriminated against by political, social, economic, and religious institutions. And despite sharing the experiences of other minorities, many of them have adopted the attitudes and stances of the dominant culture of racism, a culture that maintains control by dividing by difference and uniting by illusion of similarity. By becoming white they have paid a price, and that price is the threat to their culture. It is that near extinction of Italian American culture that has enabled them to remain invisible. But despite the efforts of many, they are not always invisible, nor can they always control when and how they are seen when they do become visible.

The murder of Yusef Hawkins in Bensonhurst is a perfect example of what it takes to make Italian Americans visible. As long as African Americans stayed out of Bensonhurst, Bensonhurst remained invisible—a small, provincial island of Italian American culture. When Yusef Hawkins walked into Bensonhurst he unfortunately was not invisible; when a dead Yusef Hawkins was carried out of Bensonhurst, the neighborhood became a visible representation of Italian America.

In *Do the Right Thing*, a film by Spike Lee, African American culture is pitted against racist American culture represented by an Italian American pizzeria owner and his sons. There are many statements made in this film, but the most powerful is that racism is as American as pizza. To become white is to buy into a racist insurance fraud. The message is, Become like us and then you too can be better than those others who cannot become like us. We'll stop racism against your people if you help us keep it alive against others.

Spike Lee chose Italians to represent American racism because he knew them as white from his experience growing up in Brooklyn, and he knew that they would not gather in numbers to protest the portrayal. I believe he also chose Italian Americans because they represented the absurdity of division between minority groups. Initial responses by Italian Americans to both the Bensonhurst murder and the Spike Lee film were defensive, divisive, and reactionary. Why portray us like that? Why use Italian Americans to demonstrate America's racist philosophy? If those who responded had just an inkling of what could be found in Italian American literature, they would have not put forth such naive notions.

Is it right? Is it fair? Is it true? These I feel are the wrong questions to ask. Like it or not there are Italian Americans who are racist, who in buying into the American dream also swallowed the American illusion that white America is better than colored America. The right questions to ask are: How can the very victims of racism adopt racist ideas? and Why don't Italian Americans present alternative views of relationships between Italian and African Americans?

A little reading of Italian American history and literature by Italian Americans will demonstrate that despite the shades of difference in skin color, Italians share much in common with other minority cultures; those commonalities have been hidden from consciousness by selective portrayals of American history. This ignorance of alternative histories is responsible for the Italian American lawyers who work to destroy labor unions that their grandparents fought and died to create and preserve. Ignorance of Italian American history invites us to regenerate a racist mentality that ensures that white will dominate.

## WE WEREN'T ALWAYS WHITE

> No one was white before he/she came to America.
> —James Baldwin, "On Being 'White'... and Other Lies"

> I'm tired of being overlooked and then categorized as colorless, as though I've never had a good spaghetti fight in my life. I'm tired of being told to shut up and assimilate.
> —Rose Romano, "Vendetta"

After the Yusef Hawkins murder, Italian American intellectuals, such as Robert Viscusi, Jerome Krase, and Marianna DeMarco Torgovnick, wrote essays and editorials that attempted to demonstrate that not all Italian Americans were racists. These essays, accompanied by the actions of New York's radical activists Italian Americans for a Multicultural United States (IAMUS), marked the beginning of a culturally critical interaction that led to the creation of larger public forums such as the 1997 American Italian Historical Association's national conference "Shades of Black and White: Conflict and Collaboration between Two Communities." (see Ashyk, Gardaphé, and Tamburri [1999]). In *Are Italians White*, Joseph Sciorra presents one of the strongest autobiographical accounts of the experience of taking part in a march protesting racism in Bensonhurst. You could not appreciate these shining moments of clarity in Italian American consciousness unless you were aware of some of the shadows cast upon Italian America by racist acts.

Reference to Black people in Mario Puzo's *The Godfather* (1969), as "dark peoples" and "animals" "who have no respect for their wives or their families or themselves" (290) is uncomfortably close to the gist of Richard Gambino's attempts to explain the differences between Italian Americans and African Americans in his 1975 *Blood of My Blood: The Dilemma of the Italian-Americans*. Gambino, one of the first to make observations about the interaction of the two communities, sees them as having "diametrically opposed value systems" (329). "It is difficult to think of two groups of Americans," he writes, "whose ways of life differ more. The two cultures are at odds with each other in superficial styles and in critical values. The groups clash more and more as ghetto blacks confront lower-middle-class whites in inner cities over efforts to integrate schools and housing and in competition for jobs and political power" (329). Confrontation is inevitable, he suggests, because the two groups often inhabit adjacent urban spaces. As evidence Gambino presents examples of how music, body language, and notions of family differ between African Americans and Italians.

A more optimistic observation was put forth by Patrick Gallo in his 1974 study *Ethnic Alienation: The Italian Americans*. Gallo saw enough similarities between Italian and African Americans to suggest the creation of an alliance of, in his words, "whites and Blacks, white-collar and blue-collar workers, based on mutual need and interdependence. . . . Italian-Americans may prove to be a vital ingredient in not only forging that alliance but in serving as the cement that will hold urban centers together" (209).

That Gambino's naive approach has gone unchallenged and Gallo's ideas have been ignored until only recently is the result of a slowly developing Italian American intelligentsia. This intelligentsia is producing a great number of poems,

stories, essays, and book-length studies that challenge Gambino's weak explanations and attempt to fulfill Gallo's prophecy. Thirteen years before either
Gambino's or Gallo's analyses appeared, Daniela Gioseffi put her body and soul
on the line in the early 1960s struggle for civil rights. She documented her experiences in a short story, "The Bleeding Mimosa" (1991), which recounts the
terror of a night spent in a Selma, Alabama, jail during which she was raped by a
southern sheriff. A recent essay by Frank Lentricchia in *Lingua Franca* reminds
us that the cultural interactions between Italian and African Americans did not
begin in response to Bensonhurst. In "Confessions of an Ex-Literary Critic,"
Lentricchia's points to Willard Motley's *Knock on Any Door* as a signal text in
his early development as a reader and writer. Lentricchia is only one of an increasing number of American writers of Italian descent who have explored the
interaction of Italian and African Americans and in the process created light by
which one can see both the discrimination against Italian Americans and the ac-
tivities they have participated in to achieve justice for all.   In a 1992 article
Robert Orsi has noted that Italian immigration occurred at the same times that
migration of African Americans from the South and African Caribbeans Italians
became part of "the first wave of dark-skinned immigrants" (316), which led to
what he calls their "inbetweeness": "The immigrants' inbetweenness and the
consequent effort to establish the border against the dark-skinned other required
an intimate struggle, a context against the initial uncertainty over which side of
the racial dichotomy the swarthy immigrants were on and against the facts of history and geography that inscribed this ambiguity on the urban landscape" (318).
Orsi's conclusion is that Italian immigrants became Italian Americans as soon as
they learned how to become white.

     In a paper presented at a 1996 Newberry Library summer seminar, David
Roediger and James R. Barrett tell us that "Italians, involved in a spectacular international Diaspora in the early twentieth century, were racialized as the
'Chinese of Europe' in many lands. But in the U. S. their racialization was pronounced, as 'guinea's' evolution suggests, more likely to connect Italians with
Africans" (Barrett and Roediger 1996, "Inbetween Peoples" 7). But the whiteness
of Italian Americans was more delayed than totally denied, and thus the danger
according to Roediger is not only swallowing the myth of white superiority, but
"being swallowed by the lie of whiteness" (quoted in Stowe 1996, 74). This danger is very real as today's Italian Americans grow up ignorant of their history and
firm in their belief of being white. As poet Diane di Prima (1996) noted in a
response to Vecoli's keynote address: "In most ways, my brothers and I were

pushed into being white, as my parents understood that term" (25), which included being forbidden to speak Italian. Di Prima argues that:

> We need to admit that this pseudo "white" identity with its present non-convenience was not something that just fell on us out of the blue, but something that many Italian Americans grabbed at with both hands. Many felt that their culture, language, food, songs, music, identity, was a small price to pay for entering American mainstream. Or they thought, like my parents probably did, that they could keep these good Italian things in private and become "white" in public. (27)

That Italian Americans could have it both ways might be seen as an advantage, but according to Noel Ignatiev, choosing whiteness means clinging to "the most serious barrier to becoming fully American" ("Immigrants and Whites," 18). Ignatiev, who with John Garvey edits the journal *Race Traitor*, presents a very radical alternative for Italian Americans: that of aiding in the abolishment of whiteness altogether. The key to making this happen is understanding how dehumanization of people is at the center of color differences constructed in the process of creating and sustaining white power and privilege. Yet Italian Americans seem to have benefited from remaining in the color controversy.

In "Italian Americans as a Cognizable Racial Group," New York State Supreme Court Justice Dominic R. Massaro (1994) surveys recent court decisions that have established Italian Americans as a racial group subject to protection by New York law, especially in cases of affirmative action. As a result of this protection, the first chair of Italian American Studies was awarded to the John D. Calandra Italian American Institute in a discrimination lawsuit against the City University of New York system. The decision in favor of the plaintiff in *Scelsa v. the City University of New York* solidified the position of Italian Americans as "inbetween people," as people capable of substantiating discrimination claims, at least in the state of New York, and as people capable of taking advantage of the privileges offered to whites. Evidence of this continues to spread across the country. Recently, Judge Massaro's article helped an Italian American professor gain a reversal in a tenure dispute in the University of California state system.

So, for Italian Americans, at least for the time being, their status as whites is flexible, perhaps flexible enough for us to refer to them as off-whites. But as Shelley Fisher Fishkin (1995) points out in a review essay on publications in whiteness studies, African American culture has always influenced American culture. "If we apply to our culture," she writes, "the 'one drop' rule that in the

United States has long classified anyone with one drop of black blood as black, then all American culture is black" ("Interrogating 'Whiteness'," 454). So, will Italian Americans remain comfortably in their inbetween status? A look at recent literature by Americans of Italian descent sheds light on the precarious position in which Italian Americans find themselves.

In *Reading Race: White American Poets and the Racial Discourse in the Twentieth Century*, Aldon Nielsen uncovers the racism implied in the works of white canonized poets of the twentieth century. Nielsen skillfully demonstrates that white American writers have, often consciously, fostered a tradition of racism in their use of language, especially in their depictions of African Americans as "the black thing." Nielsen's *Reading Race*, winner of the 1986 South Atlantic Modern Language Association Award, brings us new ways of reading traditional literature by closely observing language at work. "Our language has come to act as that metaphorical veil of which W. E. B. DuBois speaks so often, separating two national groups and occluding our vision of one another. This veil is maintained between the two terms of a racial dialectic, one of which is privileged" (1). By analyzing that "veil" Nielsen demonstrates that the images of the Black other, created by white writers, are fictions created out of the need to separate white selves from Black others. Nielsen's study provides us with a model by which we can uncover even the unconscious perpetuation of racism in modern and contemporary poetry. Racist discourse, as he tells us, is "susceptible of dissolution." And he offers Herman Melville's *Benito Cereno* as the only true example of a white writer breaking through the racist language barrier. Perhaps, most importantly, Nielsen raises the question of whether we can ever expect to "think in a language to avoid having our thought directed by the language of those from whom we learn" (163). In literature by Italian American writers, we can find examples of just the opposite of Nielsen's thesis, fictions that are created out of the need to connect Italian white selves to Black others.

Emilio DeGrazia's swan song for a disintegrating Little Italy that looms large in the mind as it shrinks on the streets of St. Paul, Minnesota, comes in his novel A *Canticle for Bread and Stones* (1997) and confronts the racist turn in Italian immigrant culture. Drawn to Minnesota to build a cathedral, Raphael Amato, the stone artist great-grandfather of protagonist Salvatore Amato, runs into trouble caused by an American philanthropist who can change minds and neighborhoods with a wave of his cash-filled hand. Salvatore searches for meaningful work in 1970s America as he tries to find out why his great-grandfather was fired from the job of building the great cathedral. This quest turns into a mystery that Salvatore must solve before he can go on with his life. The mystery takes the protagonist to several storytellers who ultimately teach him that the America he has inherited is not the same place that drew his immigrant ancestors away from the poverty of the old country.

DeGrazia's presents a "Little Italy" that was once a dream world for immigrants and has become a nightmare for subsequent generations. Salvatore's college degree never helped him find that white-collar job his parents believed would be his by rite of passage. Anchored to working-class culture, Salvatore, unlike his father, understands the economic system, wants more than a job, and is left to philosophize on the demise of Little Italy:

> Once upon a time my kind of neighborhood, full of people strolling by, shopkeepers standing in doorways when business was slow, mothers walking hand-in-hand with children distracted by some new things in a store window, old men on street corners arguing about the weather, baseball and politics, and boys weaving in and out of the sidewalk traffic so girls would see how wonderful they were. All that noise and activity gone now, nothing left but empty sidewalks and stores, here and there a yellow light shining dimly through drawn shades in an upstairs window and the slogans of sex and disgust painted on walls. At the end of the block a black woman sat head-in-hands on the curb. "Loro," Guido called them. Them. Beware of Them, the blacks moving in with their ragged mattresses and box springs and stares, this sullen people from a time so lost in space our Old World seemed new. (43)

The postimmigrant paradigm presented in DeGrazia's novel is one in which the Italian American must confront not only the silence of the past but also the silent lessons of racism that have been instilled as the immigrants learned to become white in the United States.

In her first novel Mary Bucci Bush filled a great historical void with her story of Italian American life on southern plantations during the early 1900s. Though they were called Italian colonies, to which Italians were shipped directly from Italy, many were little more than new versions of slavery. Bush's grandmother had gone to the south when she was seven years old. Though this was a common experience, very little has been published about it. Fueled by her grandmother's stories, Bush began to research the phenomenon for her novel. She found that African Americans and Italians lived next door to each other in separate plantation shacks and socialized with each other. Most of the Italians had not been farmers when they came over. "Quite often," said Bush in an unpublished conference presentation, "the Blacks taught the Italians how to survive, how to work the farm, and how to speak English." She demonstrated this in an excerpt published as a chapbook titled *Drowning*, which features the friendship between two children: One, named Isola, is the daughter of Italian immigrants; the other, Birdie, is the daughter of freed Black slaves who have become share-croppers. In the following passage, Isola divulges a secret:

> "My Papa says we all have to watch out now," Isola told Birdie.
> "What for?"
> Isola looked around. She moved closer to Birdie and
> lowered her voice. "That if we play with Nina the Americans will shoot us.
> Or maybe burn down our house." [Nina's father has led workers off the planta-
> tion in search of better work and is being chased by the owner's henchmen
> called the Gracey Men, who are members of the Ku Klux Klan.]
> Birdie took a step back and looked at Isola. "Where you got
> such a crazy idea?"
> "That's what the Gracey men do," Isola said. "That's what
> my Papa told me."
> Birdie put her hand on her hips. "You dumb or something?
> White folks don't shoot white folks." She walked faster, so that Isola had to
> trot to catch up with her.
> "But we're not white," Isola told her. "We're Italian." (11)

Bush's novel dramatizes the lack of racial separation between the two groups. "Eventually the adults did realize that the Blacks were treated different-ly," said Bush, "and were frightened by that." It wasn't until a few years after her grandmother's death that Bush tried to discover Sunnyside, the plantation that her grandmother's family had moved to in 1904. This plantation was one of many that were investigated in 1907 by the federal government because of charges of peonage. "Italian agents had worked against their own people," says Bush. "They had them sign papers, the contents of which were never truthfully explained. Some people had their passage paid by the plantation owners, but they were in-structed not to let anyone know this because it was illegal. They were told to say they were going to meet a cousin or a paesano who was paying their passage. In the end, no one was ever convicted of this peonage." Bush suggested that one explanation for this importation of Italian laborers was that white southerners, overwhelmed by the size of the Black population, wanted to diminish it by bring-ing in Italian workers. In no way, says Bush, were Italians considered to be equal to the whites. This suggestion is backed by journalistic evidence from the period.

In "The Italian Cotton Growers: The Negroes' Problem," Alfred Stone (1974), a wealthy Mississippi Delta cotton planter, expressed his hopes that the Italian, who he says has "demonstrated his superiority over the negro as an agriculturalist" (123), will continue immigrating to the South.

Another writer who complicates the whiteness of Italians is Chuck Wachtel, who is half Jewish and half Italian American. In *The Gates* (1995), we meet his protagonist, Primo Thomas, who was born to an African American doctor and his Italian American wife. While Wachtel does not spend much time on giving us the details of Primo's mixed ancestry, he reminds us that while there are many ways in which these two cultures are different, there are many more in which they're similar. In a subtle stroke, Wachtel uses the vegetable eggplant, which in Italian has a double meaning (*melanzane* is a term used to refer to black-skinned people), to have Primo both acknowledge his Italianness and the racism he experiences from Italian Americans. When Primo and his friends attend a Saint Anthony festa in Little Italy, an Italian American family is staring at him in obvious hatred. Primo walks up to the family and says, "When my mother made 'moolinyam,' she'd never used too much cheese. She used to say real Italians know that God made eggplant so you could taste it, not disguise the flavor ..." And then turning to the daughter, he continues, "My mother also used to say that the dark, shiny skin of an eggplant was beautiful. It was a mystery to her how anyone could make a bad word out of something so beautiful. She liked to kiss my arms when she said it. Your mother ever kiss your arms?" (15). While Primo's black skin might keep others from recognizing his Italianness, his memory of his mother, sustained through his Aunt Olivia, keeps him connected to a past that continues to nurture him long after his parents have died.

Nonidentification with white culture is the theme of Anthony Valerio's (1996) "Water for Toni Morrison," published in *Voices in Italian Americana*. Valerio recounts, in his trademark mix of fiction and nonfiction, an encounter with the Nobel Prize-winning African American author. Through the character Gloria Lewis (the pseudonym for a famous Black writer with whom Valerio had a relationship) Valerio learns about Morrison's life and the pain that doesn't get transmitted during her public presentations. Knowing what he does about her private life, Valerio writes: "Being the unfortunate Italian that I am, I felt proud, blessed that this pain had passed from Toni Morrison to Gloria Lewis down to me, from women to a man, from Black women to an Olive man" (99). The story flashes from the protagonist's inner thoughts that come while watching Morrison being interviewed by Charlie Rose on public television to the time when he accompanies Lewis to a film screening reception attended by Morrison. At that reception, Morrison asks for a glass of water, and Valerio, whom Gloria Lewis had nicknamed Rio, is assigned the task of fetching it. With all the gallantry of Don Quixote combined with the practicality of Sancho Panza, Valerio turns a simple errand into a quest. Because he thought he "had to be a man among Blacks," he is without his usual leather shoulder bag that his Bensonhurst aunt told him only girls carried; this bag "had everything anybody needed right there. Rubber bands, paper clips, matches, flyers, pencils, pennies—things picked up on the street" because he had learned "that big people sometimes need little things. That what one person throws away, another person needs. This was one way people connect" (102).

As the protagonist is in search for the water, there is a flashback to the television interview. When the conversation comes around to racism, Valerio is horrified and embarrassed "when she said that when Italians came here, they became white. I have known more Italians than Blacks, perhaps less intimately in a sexual sense, socially to be sure, and not one Italian in the dark recesses feels white" (103). After he returns from his quest with two paper cups of water, the narrative returns to the interview and Morrison's first recollection of racism. "In her grammar school in the landlocked Midwest, she had a friend, a little Italian girl, and little Toni Morrison had taught her friend how to read and then one day the Italian came to school and would not go near her" (103). And with that, Valerio leaves the Morrison interview and returns to the reception and the last time he and Gloria Lewis were together with Toni Morrison. The juxtaposition of the story of his water boy errand to Morrison's earliest recollection of racism serves as a baptism of sorts through which not only the protagonist but all Italian Americans can be washed of the sins of racism by realizing the absurdity of it all.

More militant in her attempt to avoid being white is poet and publisher Rose Romano. In her essay "Coming Out Olive in the Lesbian Community: Big Sister Is Watching," Romano (1996) argues that respect in the lesbian community is gained through recognition of one's suffering, which depends on skin color: "The lighter one's skin, the less respect one is entitled to" (161). "I have been told that by calling myself Olive I am evading my 'responsibility of guilt.' Because I am a light-skinned woman living in the United States, it is accepted that my grandparents, whether they owned slaves themselves, belonged to the group who did own slaves and were entitled to all the benefits. If they chose not to take advantage of those benefits, it's their own fault. When I tell lesbians that Southern Italians and Sicilians didn't even begin to arrive in this country until twenty years after the slave days were over, I am told that this is a 'wrong use of facts' and that today I am a member of an oppressor group and that I can choose to take advantage of my 'white-skin privilege.'" Unable to gain respect for her own experiences, Romano criticizes the lesbian publishing community for denying access to Italian American writers.

Nicholas Montemarano brings Italian American racism to the fore in his novel *A Fine Place* (2002) by dramatizing a Hawkins-like killing from the point of view of Bensonhurst's Italian Americans. What's powerful in this novel is Montemarano's contemplation of the unnatural. We meet few people in this novel, which revolves around the lives of Vera and Sal Santangelo, their son Gino, his wife Josephine, and their son Tony who is the one labeled as the murderer. Though three generations share the same environment, they all face different realities. "But what did *they* know of this neighborhood, thought Tony. They knew the market and the Italian delicatessen. They knew the price of chop meat at the butcher. They knew who was engaged, who was pregnant, who was sick, who was dying. They knew every crack in the sidewalk. But what did they *know*? The pool hall, for example. Did they know that there were fights there every night, always between Italians, usually about girls?" Tony is speaking about the generation that taught him to be racist, and, as the novel reveals, it was this self-protecting insularity that fostered the fear of others, outsiders, Black people. Tony, fortified in his racist upbringing, takes this fear to its absurd height by participating in the murder, but it is Tony, in the end, who confronts his racism by carrying around a black brick that was once tossed through his window. The brick becomes like the albatross of *The Rime of the Ancient Mariner*; Tony's life is reduced to the story of how he became separated from his neighborhood, identified as the killer, and vilified for life. No matter where he goes, the story will proceed and define him for as long as he lives.

With *Italian American: The Racializing of and Ethnic Identity*, David A. J. Richards (1999) brings a more legalistic perspective to the discussion of Italians and whiteness. Richards, a grandson of Italian immigrants who came from the hill towns of Campania, sheds light on how American racism kept Italian Americans from knowing "both their own traditions in Italy and the very real struggles of their grandparents against injustice in both Italy and the United States" (6–7). Richards draws on cases of race, women's, and sexual-preference rights as he interprets "moral slavery," the backfiring of a racism created by the denial of basic human rights to people who are dehumanized so that those rights can be denied. Richards concludes his study by offering a "rights-based protest" to counter the effects of moral slavery. Such a protest consists of first "claiming rights denied in one's own voice" and then "engaging in reasonable discourse that challenges the dominant stereotype in terms of which one's group has been dehumanized" (214). Richards calls for us all to see that "It is no longer an acceptable basis for any people's Americanization that they subscribe to the terms of American cultural racism" (236). This is precisely what is done by the authors I have presented in this essay.[2]

Mary Bucci Bush, Chuck Wachtel, Anthony Valerio, Rose Romano, Nicholas Montemarano, and David Richards are just a few of American writers of Italian descent who, in the words of Noel Ignatiev and John Garvey, are "race traitors." They are joined by the late poet and *Sparrow* publisher Felix Stefanile (1992), whose poem "Hubie" recounts the integration of his "eyetalian" Army unit in World War II and his friendship with a Black soldier. In this poem Stefanile tells us that after the war came another war: "A black man and a white man, that's for sure,/ this other war, and the cagey cowardice/ of habit, turning honest blood to ice./ I think that we were brothers once, "The Twins,"/ the fellows called us, masking their wide grins./ What's left is poetry, the penance for my sins (77)." The penance is the recognition that outside of the army, the "Twins" could never share the same experiences again. Such identification with African Americans abounds. In Frank Lentricchia's (1994) imaginative auto-fiction *The Edge of Night*, the author creates a character who avenges JFK's murder in the guise of "a multicultural avenger, the black Italian-American Othello," who contains "all the best of dark and bright" and "croons out of the black part of my soul, Has anyone here seen my old friend Martin" (165)? Prior to his death in January of 1992, Pietro di Donato, author of *Christ in Concrete*, completed a controversial, unpublished novel titled *The American Gospels*, in which Christ, in the form of a Black woman, comes to Earth at the end of the world to pass judgment on key historical figures of contemporary America.

As I hope to have shown, the interaction between Italians and African Americans is more complex than earlier scholars have suggested, and the literature produced by Italian American writers contains the fuel to fire the slogan of whiteness studies coined by Ignatiev and Garvey: "Treason to whiteness is loyalty to humanity." This treason is evidenced by Lucia Chiavola Birnbaum's (1993) study *Black Madonnas*, which makes a case for intercultural interdependence on images of what Italians refer to as *La Madonna nera*, or the black Madonna, and her latest work-in-progress, *Dark Mothers: African Origins and Godmothers* (2002). Birnbaum's groundbreaking research earned her induction into the African American Multicultural Educators Hall of Fame in 1996. The treason also exists in films such as Chaz Palminteri's screenplay for *A Bronx Tale*, which became a film directed by Robert DeNiro, which depicts a young Italian American who falls in love with a Black girl. If not totally Black, Italians have certainly complicated the notion of whiteness in America so that they are not totally white, and it is this in-between status that makes them likely candidates for assisting in the abolition of whiteness in the United States.

## Works Cited and Selected Readings

Ashyk, Dan, Fred Gardaphé, and Anthony Tamburri. 1999. *Shades of Black and White: Conflict and Collaboration between Two Communities*. Staten Island, NY: The American Italian Historical Association.

Baldwin, James. 1984. "On Being 'White'... and Other Lies." *Essence*. (April): 90–92.

Barrett, James R. and David Roediger. "Inbetween Peoples: Race, Nationality and the 'New Immigrant' Working Class." Paper Presented at the Newberry Library, Summer.

Belliotti, Raymond A. 1995. *Seeing Identity: Individualism Versus Community in an Ethnic Context*. Lawrence, KS: University Press of Kansas.

Birnbaum, Lucia Chiavola. 1993. *Black Madonnas: Feminism, Religion, and Politics in Italy*. Boston: Northeastern University Press.

Birnbaum, Lucia Chiavola. 2002. *Dark Mothers: African Origins and Godmothers*. New York: Author's Choice Press.

Bona, Mary Jo and Anthony Julian Tamburri, Eds. Staten Island, NY: American Italian Historical Association. 24–29.

Bush, Mary Bucci. 1994. "Planting." *The Voices We Carry: Short Fiction by Italian American Women*. Mary Jo Bona, Ed. Montreal: Guernica Editions. 33–56.

di Prima, Diane. 1996. "'Don't Solidify the Adversary!' A Response to Rudolph Vecoli." *Through the Looking Glass: Italian and Italian/American Images in the Media*. Selected Essays from the 27th Annual Conference of the American Italian Historical Association.

Fishkin, Shelley Fisher. 1995. "Interrogating 'Whiteness,' 'Complicating 'Blackness:' Remapping American Culture." *American Quarterly*. 47.3 (September): 428–536.

Gallo, Patrick J. 1974. *Ethnic Alienation: The Italian-Americans*. Cranbury, NJ: Associated University Presses.

Gambino, Richard. 1975. *Blood of My Blood. The Dilemma of the Italian American*. New York: Anchor.

Gardaphe, Fred L. 2002. We Weren't Always White." *LIT*. 13.3 (July-September): 185–199.

Gioseffi, Daniela. 1991. "The Bleeding Mimosa." *Voices in Italian American*. 2.1: 59–65.

Ignatiev, Noel. 1996. "Immigrants and Whites." *Race Traitor*. Noel Ignatiev and John Garvey, Eds. New York: Routledge. 15–23.

Krase, Jerome. 1994. "Bensonhurst, Brooklyn: Italian-American Victimizers and Victims." *Voices in Italian Americana*. 5.2 (Fall): 43–53.

Krase, Jerome. 1996. "New Approaches to the Study of Italian Americans in Metropolitan New York." *Italian Americans on Long Island: Presence and Impact*. Kenneth P. LaValle, Ed. Stony Brook, NY: Filibrary. 32–51.

LaGumina, Salvatore J. 1973. *Wop! A Documentary History of Anti-Italian Discrimination in the United States*. San Francisco: Straight Arrow Books.

Lentricchia, Frank. 1994. *The Edge of Night*. New York: Random House.

Lentricchia, Frank. 1999. *Music of the Inferno*. Albany, NY: State University of New York Press.

Massaro, Dominic R. 1994. "Italian Americans as a Cognizable Racial Group." *Italian Americans in a Multicultural Society*. Proceedings of the Symposium of the

American Italian Historical Association, 1993. *Forum Italicum*: SUNY, Stonybrook, NY. 44–55.

Montemarano, Nick. 2002. *A Fine Place*. New York: Context Books.

Moquin, Wayne, Ed. 1974. *A Documentary History of the Italian Americans*. New York: Praeger.

Novak, Michael. 1996. *Unmeltable Ethnics: Politics and Culture in American Life*. Second Edition. New Brunswick, NJ: Transaction Publishers.

Orsi, Robert Anthony. 1992. "The Religious Boundaries of an Inbetween People: Street Feste and the Problem of the Dark-Skinned Other in Italian Harlem, 1920–1990." *American Quarterly*. 44.3 (September): 313–347.

Parini, Jay and Ciongoli, Kenneth. 1997. Beyond "The Godfather:" *Italian American Writers on the Real Italian American Experience*. Hanover, NH: University Press of New England.

Puzo, Mario. 1969. *The Godfather*. New York. Fawcett.

Richards. David A. J. 1999. *Italian American: The Racializing of an Ethnic Identity*. New York: New York University Press.

Roediger, David. 1994. *Toward the Abolition of Whiteness*. New York: Verso.

Romano, Rose. 1990. *Vendetta*. San Francisco: malafemmina press.

Romano, Rose. 1993. "Vendetta." *la Bella Figura: A Choice*. Rose Romano, Ed. San Francisco: malafemmina press. 35–42.

Romano, Rose. 1994. *The Wop Factor*. Brooklyn/Palermo: malafemmina press.

Romano, Rose. 1996. "Coming Out Olive in the Lesbian Community: Big Sister is Watching." *Social Pluralism and Literary History: The Literature of the Italian Emigration*.

Francesco Loriggio, Ed. Toronto: Guernica Editions. 161–175.

Stefanile, Felix. 1992. "Hubie." *The Dance at St. Gabriel's*. Brownsville, OR: Story Line Press. 158.

Stone, Alfred. 1974. "The Italian Cotton Growers: The Negroes' Problem." *South Atlantic Quarterly*. (January 1905). Reprinted in *A Documentary History of Italian Americans*. Wayne Moquin, Ed. New York: Praeger. 122–125.

Stowe, David W. 1996. "Uncolored People: The Rise of Whiteness Studies." *Lingua Franca*. (September-October): 68–77.

Takaki, Ronald. 1993. *A Different Mirror*. New York: Little Brown & Co.

Tamburri, Anthony Julian, Paolo A. Giordano, and Fred L. Gardaphé, Eds. 1991. *From the Margin: Writings in Italian Americana*. West Lafayette, IN: Purdue University Press.

Torgovnick, Marianna DeMarco. 1994. "On Being White, Female, and Born in Bensonhurst." *Crossing Ocean Parkway: Readings by an Italian American Daughter*. Chicago: University of Chicago Press. 3–18.

Valerio, Anthony. 1996. "Water for Toni Morrison." *Voices in Italian Americana*. 7.1(Spring): 99–104.

Vecoli, Rudolph J. 1996. "'Are Italian Americans Just White Folks?'" *Through the Looking Glass: Italian and Italian/American Images in the Media*. Selected Essays from the 27th Annual Conference of the American Italian Historical Association. Mary Jo Bona and Anthony Julian Tamburri, Eds. Staten Island, NY: American Italian Historical Association. 3–17.

Viscusi, Robert. 1990. "Breaking the Silence: Strategic Imperatives for Italian American Culture." *Voices in Italian Americana*. 1.1, 1–14.

Wachtel, Chuck. 1995. *The Gates*. New York: Viking/Penguin.

# "A Real Easygoing Place"/ "A Place for Rushing Through": Race, Music, and the Mob in the 1950s French Quarter

GEORGE DE STEFANO

> Let's fly down or drive down to New Orleans/That city has pretty
> historic scenes/I'll take you parade you down Bourbon Street/There's
> a lot of hot spots/you'll see lots of big shots/ down on Bourbon Street.
> —Paul Barbarin, "Bourbon Street Parade"

## "WHAT WOULD BOURBON STREET LOOK LIKE IF IT WERE NOT FOR THE SICILIANS?"

Richard Campanella's rhetorical question points to a historical fact: Sicilians were instrumental in developing New Orleans's most famous and lucrative entertainment district (De Stefano 2014). Sicilian immigrants began to settle in large numbers in the French Quarter around the turn of the twentieth century. Although many were desperately poor and lived in cramped, deteriorating housing, entrepreneurs soon arose among the inhabitants of "Little Palermo" who opened restaurants, bars, nightclubs, and music venues. Campanella, a professor of architecture and geography at Tulane University and the author of numerous books about New Orleans, says that Sicilians constituted "at least a plurality and usually a majority among Bourbon and [French] Quarter business and building owners, and more than any other group they deserve credit, or blame, for creating modern Bourbon Street" (Campanella 2014, 147–148).

Bourbon Street comprises thirteen blocks in the French Quarter and one in Marigny, across Esplanade Avenue. It is about half residential and half commercial; most bars, nightclubs, music venues, and strip clubs have been concentrated on its upper blocks, toward Canal Street. The street's history began in 1722, when Adrien de Pauger, an engineer in the employ of the French monarchy, gave it its exact location, length, width, block, and parcel delineations (Campanella 2014, 15). New Orleans passed from France to Spain late in the eighteenth century while remaining mainly Francophone and Caribbean culturally. But with the waning of its empire, Spain ceded Louisiana to France. Napoleon Bonaparte, concerned about imperial overreach and needing funds, sold Louisiana to the

United States in 1803 for $15 million. After the Louisiana Purchase, New Orleans officially became a US city.

In the early 1800s, Bourbon Street's population was working- and middle-class, with small businesses. By the middle of the century, its ethnic composition was 66 percent French and 17 percent English, with single-digit percentages of Italian, German, Spanish, Jewish, and Portuguese (Campanella 2014, 39). The French Opera House was built during this period, at the corner of Bourbon and Toulouse Streets. It was one of the city's most popular cultural institutions until it was destroyed in a fire in 1919. Bourbon Street's shift to an entertainment and tourist attraction began in the early 1900s; new hotels were built for visitors and old ones adapted to the burgeoning tourist trade. The neighborhood's ethnic mix also began to change; although the French Creole population remained, in the early 1900s "the top three languages spoken in the French Quarter were now American English, New Orleans French, and Sicilian Italian" (95).

Many "respectable" bourgeois New Orleanians regarded the French Quarter, particularly Bourbon Street, as disreputable and even dangerous. After New Orleans closed Storyville, the city's legal red-light district, in 1917, the sex trade flourished in the Quarter and on Bourbon Street. From 1917–1919, Bourbon Street was "well-positioned to control the new business of bacchanal" (Campanella 2014, 100). Soldiers on their way to European battlefronts or returning home from the war made up most of the clientele of the neighborhood's prostitutes. Bourbon Street's bacchanalia might have made the area internationally known in the Roaring Twenties, except for the temperance movement. Louisiana's anti-alcohol efforts began with a "local option" on alcohol control granted in 1902. Seven years later, the Louisiana legislature passed the Gay-Shattuck Law, which targeted not only drinking but the social milieux in which New Orleanians drank and partied. In a reactionary state like Louisiana that had codified white suprem-acy into Jim Crow law, restricted women's legal rights and access to public venues, and exhibited animus toward Sicilian immigrants, it's not surprising that the Gay-Shattuck law would have particular consequences for Black people, women, and Sicilians. Some consequences, however, were unintended by the legislature's conservative guardians of public morality.

Gay-Shattuck segregated Black people and whites to separate bars, prohibit-ed women from venues that sold alcohol, and banned musical performances and even the presence of musical instruments in establishments where liquor was sold. Violations were punishable by a fine of $50 to $500 or a jail term not ex-ceeding two years. But the law did not bar women, alcohol, musicians, and performances from establishments that served food, such as restaurants or hotels.

"Mixed company, cuisine, libations, musical entertainment: these were all the key ingredients to a 'club.' And because few people drink and dance during the daytime, the enterprise became a 'night' club" (Campanella 2014, 100).

Enforcement of the law fell heavily on Sicilians in the French Quarter. Their corner grocery stores often also functioned as bars, and in those and other establishments, Sicilians served Black customers, flouting the racial segregation mandated by Gay-Shattuck. Records from the Criminal District Court for the Parish of Orleans are replete with the names of Sicilians arrested for violating Gay-Shattuck, one indication of their resistance to the law. A few sample citations will suffice. In 1914, "One Santo Greco and one Joseph Sale" were prosecuted because "each did then and there conduct a barroom and drinking saloon" and "did sell and permit to be sold . . . intoxicating liquors to persons of the white or Caucasian race and to persons of the colored or negro race." In 1915, Jake Guarisco and Tony Terranova were prosecuted for the same offense, as were Alfred Ragusa and Elwood Ragusa the following year. There were many more such prosecutions of Sicilian business owners under Gay-Shattuck.

Louisiana's law was one of the numerous attempts nationwide to restrict alcohol consumption. Not only did Gay-Shattuck encourage defiance; it also had the unintended consequence of spurring the emergence of a new type of entertainment venue, the nightclub. Then in 1920 the United States prohibited the manufacture, sale, and transportation of alcoholic beverages. Prohibition—imposed on Americans by "WASP zealots of sobriety," as Gay Talese called the prohibitionists (De Stefano 2010)—encouraged defiance on a much greater scale than Gay-Shattuck. New Orleanians who patronized Sicilian-owned establishments resisted its enforcement, sometimes violently. In a restaurant owned by Felix Tranchino, a customer hit a prohibition agent in the head with a bottle; the agent fired his gun, causing panicked patrons to flee. Even such a prominent businessperson as Frank Monteleone, co-owner of the Monteleone Hotel, fell afoul of Prohibition: He was arrested in 1923 for carrying a bottle of liquor wrapped in a newspaper (Jackson 1978, 269).

Prohibition ended on December 5, 1933, with the repeal of the Eighteenth Amendment to the US Constitution. Bourbon Street's bars and other drinking establishments no longer had to worry about visits from federal agents who might close them down. (These booze-serving businesses remained racially segregated, however.) By the 1940s, Sicilians owned most establishments presenting live music in the French Quarter and nearby Tremé. Nightlife was thriving thanks to an influx of tourists after World War II. Nightclub owners were mainly men of Sicilian descent. Two popular Sicilian-owned establishments, Steve Valenti's

Paddock Lounge and Sid Davilla's Mardi Gras Lounge, specialized in traditional New Orleans jazz (Souther 2006, 46). Michael Tessitore's Caldonia Inn was a bar and music club patronized by Black people that presented such acts as the blues singer and guitarist Earl King and a pianist who would become one of New Orleans's greatest and most beloved artists: Henry Roeland Byrd. In October 2017, I shared drinks and conversation by the pool of the Hotel Richelieu with Tessitore's grandson Mike, then in his early seventies, as he reminisced about his grandfather and the club scene of the post–World War II era. He recalled how his *nonno* hired Henry Roeland Byrd in 1948 and gave him his stage name: Professor Longhair. In Storyville, New Orleans's red-light district, the pianists who played in bordellos were known as "professors." The sobriquet stuck even after the federal government shut down Storyville in 1917. "My grandfather told me he said to [Byrd], 'You're a professor of the piano. You have that long hair. You are Professor Longhair'" (De Stefano 2017c).

> I remember meeting the Professor as a young boy and going to the Caldonia. He'd be rehearsing sometimes, and he came to my grandfather's house one time. Brought him some fish and stuff. They had a good relationship. And my grandfather would tell me about him. He said he was so good that not only could he play, but he could write and sing. He said he could write a song about anything. He said the Professor wrote a song about a hole in the ground. I said, "You can't!" And my grandfather said, "Well, he did." For years I searched for that song, and I found it on a rare album.

It was mostly Italians who owned all of the clubs, "especially the Black clubs," Mike said. "I don't know, maybe some of that was mob influence or whatever, but it was run right. Tourists were treated right. Nobody was getting hurt on Bourbon Street."

Jeannine Matranga Ickes, born in New Orleans in 1939, concurs with Tessitore's characterization of the French Quarter's entertainment scene. "I can tell you that, in the '50s, New Orleans was a great place to grow up for a person like me. Lots of fun," she recalled. "We spent lots of time as teenagers in the French Quarter. It was wide open. Nobody ever asked for an ID or anything like that. It was a real easygoing place" (De Stefano 2016a).

Tessitore's and Matranga Icke's fond memories notwithstanding, behind the flashy façade and freewheeling atmosphere of the French Quarter and its Bourbon Street scene lurked two social evils that would endure for decades: racial segregation and organized crime. As Tessitore's comment about the Quarter having been "run right" suggests, the "mob influence" was crucial to ensuring that white folks like Jeannine Matranga Ickes could enjoy themselves in Bourbon Street's segregated venues.

For Black people, the French Quarter was not "the real easygoing place" it was for Jeannine Matranga Ickes. Although she and other white New Orleanians have fond memories, "most blacks either had no interest in visiting an urban space they viewed as a white attraction or did not wish to risk harassment by the New Orleans police" (Souther 2006, 76). The Quarter "was a place where blacks worked as cooks, dishwashers, porters, bellhops, musicians, and domestics"—not spent leisure time. In *The Yellow House*, her memoir about growing up poor and Black in New Orleans, Sarah M. Broom writes, "For all of my life, the French Quarter was a place where I and many of my siblings worked, a place for rushing through, and certainly not a place where we might live and sleep at night" (Broom 2019, 300).

Bars and clubs featured Black musicians, but under Jim Crow, they were segregated. Blacks didn't venture into white venues, and whites rarely patronized majority Black ones. (However, "some intrepid white tourists journeyed to black clubs in dilapidated wards beyond the tidy precincts of the Vieux Carré" [Souther 2006, 77]). A 1956 statute prohibiting interracial contact in public accommodations gave police license to raid bars and clubs with mixed clientele. The measure even forbade Black and white musicians from sharing the stage in bars and clubs. "When enforcing the law against integrated bands, policemen concentrated on the French Quarter, the urban space most visible to white natives and tourists" (78).

White-owned clubs—which is to say, mainly Sicilian-owned—were "at best drafty places for black customers in the postwar years," writes Charles Suhor (2001) in his history of New Orleans jazz from the late 1940s to 1970. That would seem to be an understatement. During the 1950s, segregation "was in full force in New Orleans . . . and that was the case on Bourbon Street as well. African Americans were not welcome on the strip or in the establishments as patrons—nor were they able to walk down the street itself without harassment" (Walker 2020). The law prohibiting Black and white musicians from playing together "discouraged varied and sustained musical interaction." Suhor cites the example of Sicilian American saxophonist Al Belletto and Black drummer Earl Palmer being arrested for jamming together in a private house in the French Quarter. He maintains, however, that despite "some notable crackdowns on integrated musical performances," New Orleans police didn't have a "coherent policy" in enforcing segregation law (Suhor 2001, 8). Suhor notes several instances of Black and white musicians performing together in the 1950s at "major downtown hotels" and other public venues. "In a policy-driven environment, raids, arrests, and prosecutions would have been routine. In retrospect, we might infer that police policy went something like this: lean only on those who lack a semblance of public support, and only if it's politically useful to do so" (Suhor 2001, 9).

Whether enforcement of segregation was routine or selective, Jim Crow's heavy hand often fell on New Orleans's premier Black entertainment venue, the Dew Drop Inn. The nightclub presented top national performers—among them Duke Ellington, Nat King Cole, James Brown, Ike and Tina Turner, Otis Redding, and Sam Cooke—and such New Orleans eminences as Allen Toussaint, Irma Thomas, Earl King, James Booker, Earl Palmer, and Huey "Piano" Smith. The club's owner, Frank Painia, an African American former barber from Plaquemines Parish, served Black and white customers in the same room, which earned him "continual police harassment and even arrests" (Hart 2021). In 1952, nine whites were arrested at the Dew Drop "for being white while drinking." By the decade's end, white people had to obtain "special police permission to interact with blacks in black-only places or else risk charges of disturbing the public order." Black people "could gain no such permission to enter white establishments" (Campanella 2014, 150).

Many of the musicians working on Bourbon Street were Black, as was most of the music being performed in its clubs and bars—jazz, rhythm and blues, rock 'n' roll. Many of the era's Black artists also were recording hit singles and albums in Cosimo Matassa's studios. Black musicians who worked in Bourbon Street venues recall the indignities they endured—having to enter the places they worked through back doors and taking their breaks in back rooms or side streets—and worse. White New Orleanians in the 1950s may have "idolized black musicians as superstars," but they "also applauded when those same musicians were beaten and robbed by cops whenever they walked around Bourbon Street without prominently displaying their instruments" (Brouillette and Randazzo 2009, 92).

Deacon John Moore, a popular rhythm and blues and jazz singer, says that in clubs owned by "Italian families," Black musicians "couldn't go into a bar and mingle with [white] patrons." "During your break, you had to stay in the green room before or after the set. You couldn't sit at the bar or talk with girls." "When desegregation came, club and bar owners designated their venues as 'key clubs,' private clubs, as a way to exclude black people. They'd be asked if they had a key, which they didn't. Even after the 1964 civil rights law passed, people didn't voluntarily comply. Club owners were afraid that black people would come in and they'd lose white customers" (De Stefano 2017b). When I mentioned Deacon John's comments to Mike Tessitore, he said, "I think it was like that." His partner

Linda, who accompanied him to our interview, remarked, "It was exactly like that" (De Stefano 2017c). Richard Campanella observes that it wasn't only Sicilian establishments that practiced racial segregation. "The owners of the Roosevelt Hotel and The Royal Orleans, the first of the big modern hotels, built in 1960, all were upholding Jim Crow" (De Stefano 2014). But the trajectory from Sicilians defying Gay-Shattuck to enforcing segregation can be seen as a metaphor for their "whitening" in the decades after they immigrated and settled in southern Louisiana.

Once legal barriers to integrated performances were struck down in the mid-1960s, mixed bands appeared more frequently. Al Belletto in 1964 "presented the first highly visible, full-time integrated combo in the city" when he was musical director of the Playboy Club (Suhor 2001, 237). The city's two musicians unions, the white Local 174 and the Black Local 496, were formally integrated five years later. These developments did not mean that racism had been eliminated from the Bourbon Street scene. Some club owners continued to oppose integrated performances, and some white musicians felt threatened by the advantages they had enjoyed for years under Jim Crow.

Besides integration, another development fostered a more progressive environment for musicians and particularly for jazz. In the immediate postwar years, numerous musicians, mostly white, found employment and opportunities to jam in French Quarter strip clubs. Bourbon Street venues featured strippers with names like Cat Girl, Evangeline the Oyster Girl, Champagne Girl, Miss Amazon, Alouette Le Blanc, the Tassel Spinner, and celebrity strippers like Blaze Starr. Louisiana governor Earl Long's well-publicized affair with Starr "helped make Long, Starr, Bourbon Street, and Louisiana all the more delectably notorious to the national consciousness" (Campanella 2014, 152).

By the late 1950s, strip clubs vastly outnumbered jazz venues, and a highly competitive market for strippers emerged on Bourbon Street. Another group of performers found work on Bourbon Street: musicians, who found steady and reasonably well-paying jobs, ranging from "neophytes" and "vagabonds" who drifted in and out of the entertainment scene to those who accompanied the bump-and-grind artists, to jobbing musicians organized into unions, to celebrity artists like Al Hirt and Pete Fountain, who owned their clubs (Campanella 2014, 152). In the 1940s, these places typically were seedy and the dancing amateurish. B-girls and prostitutes "worked the dark, ill-smelling rooms, soliciting watered-down drinks and sometimes 'rolling' hapless customers (i.e., robbing them after drugging or clobbering them)." In the 1950s, some clubs began to upgrade the strip shows, hiring famous ecdysiasts like Blaze Starr and Sally Rand and others who had gimmicks that drew in customers, like the above-mentioned Lily Christine the Cat Girl and Evangeline the Oyster Girl. Some of these clubs hired jazz musicians, including Al Belletto, Earl Palmer, and Louis Prima's bandleader Sam Butera. Two great modernists who were not New Orleans natives, guitarist Joe Pass and pianist Bill Evans, worked their trade in the bump-and-grind houses. Modern jazz, with "its heavily accented phrases and 'weird' harmonies, became part of the decidedly countercultural, borderline verboten ambiance." Given that most other venues offered only traditional New Orleans jazz, "many modern jazz artists chose to make a living in the strip clubs" (Suhor 2001, 207).

In 1964, district attorney Jim Garrison launched a crackdown on the French Quarter strip joints and other venues as part of an anticorruption campaign. Garrison is best known for his conspiracy theories about the assassination of President John F. Kennedy and his prosecution of New Orleans businessman Clay Shaw in that context, which ended with Shaw's acquittal. Oliver Stone made Garrison a crusading hero in his meretricious film *JFK*, starring Kevin Costner. In his memoir of his life as a mobbed-up French Quarter pimp, *Mr. New Orleans*, Frenchy Brouillette describes Garrison as "one of nature's authentically strange motherfuckers: a 6'7" bisexual sex maniac with a big melon head and an obsessive hunger for hookers, swinger orgies, and picking up drag queens in the French Quarter." As if anticipating his readers' raised eyebrows, Brouillette adds, "How do I know? Because he was my fucking customer for years" (Brouillette and Randazzo 2009, 127).

In Brouillette and Randazzo's (2009) account, Garrison was too afraid of New Orleans mob boss Carlos Marcello to target Marcello's bookies and gambling dens and too compromised by his patronage of prostitutes to crack down on the French Quarter bordellos. So, he focused on the bars where B-girls and strippers worked. Charles Suhor (2001) observes that Garrison's crackdown had a positive effect, as former strip-club owners turned their businesses into music venues.

Mac Rebennack, who cut his musician's teeth in French Quarter clubs before his success as Dr. John, remembers things differently. Garrison, he writes in his memoir *Under a Hoodoo Moon*, "came in and started padlocking everything—gambling joints, whorehouses, the works" (Rebennack 1994, 112). Nightlife "wasn't closed down just on Bourbon Street; it was all over the place—St. Charles Avenue, La Salle Street, music strips up and down Canal Street and out in Jefferson and St. Bernard parishes" (113). Since "live gigs and vice went hand in hand," musicians found it increasingly difficult to find work. Rebennack says that with Garrison's crackdown, many musicians he knew left New Orleans for opportunities elsewhere—Los Angeles, New York, Memphis, and Chicago (113).

Brouillette and Randazzo's *Mr. New Orleans* may not be entirely dependable as a factual account. In an introductory note, Matthew Randazzo acknowledges that the book is "an unapologetically imperfect historical document, where corroborated truth is filed next to hard-to-believe and impossible-to-verify stories of ancient gangland mayhem" (Brouillette and Randazzo 2009, vii). But for sheer raunchiness, name-dropping candor, and unapologetic nostalgia for French Quarter vice, nothing comes close to *Mr. New Orleans*. Brouillette's book (the writing was by Randazzo) depicts the French Quarter as an adult playground run by mobsters and their associates. In his 1950s heyday, it "was a beautiful place to live if you don't mind sharing your neighborhood with hundreds of pimps, gangsters, and crazies" (68). Back then, the Quarter "was not just a tourist trap" but a community akin to "a tiny, homey, and somewhat deranged nineteenth-century village in the center of a modern city" (68).

Brouillette's French Quarter was Mafia territory, run by Sicilian gangsters: "The ultimate French Quarter insider was the mafioso" (Brouillette and Randazzo 2009, 68). From the late 1940s to the 1980s, the organized crime boss of New Orleans (and territories beyond the city) was Carlos Marcello. He was born Calogero Minicori in Tunisia in 1910 to Sicilian parents from Ravenusa, a town in Agrigento province. He and his family moved to Louisiana when he was a baby, settling in Algiers, the only part of Orleans Parish on the West Bank of the Mississippi River. The family worked on a plantation until they could afford to buy a farm in the Algiers swampland. As a boy, Carlos sold their produce in the French Market in New Orleans but soon turned to crime. At nineteen, he was convicted of robbing a grocery store and sentenced to prison. From those humble beginnings, he built a vast and lucrative empire that included illegal and legal businesses.

Frenchy Brouillette was introduced to Marcello by a French Quarter racketeer who thought that Brouillette, a young, muscular Cajun from the countryside, had potential as a criminal, which he would fulfill as a pimp and "a hard-living runner for the South's most powerful bookmaking syndicate," controlled by Marcello (Brouillette and Randazzo 2009, 60). Brouillette describes Marcello, who was known as the "Little Man," as "a five-foot-four, Humpty Dumpty little dago with silver and black hair" who "so radiated power and aggression that I felt myself grow smaller with each step I took toward him" (84).

According to Brouillette, the Little Man also was "the first African American mob boss." Understanding his personality required "coming to terms with his blackness, or at least what he feared would be seen as his blackness." Brouillette describes Marcello as being as culturally Black as he was Sicilian. The diminutive mobster "talked jive, partied in jazz clubs, wore enormous black sunglasses in the dead of night and knew more black folk on a first-name basis than any pandering politician" (Brouillette and Randazzo 2009, 88). Thanks mainly to his including records by Black artists in the jukeboxes he forced bars and clubs to install, Marcello helped spread the blues throughout the South. He established his first headquarters in a Black bar, where he sold marijuana and moonshine.

Yet despite his apparent affinity for Black people and culture, "whenever Carlos was around white folk, he acted like black people gave him hives," peppering his speech with racial slurs, bragging that he donated to the Ku Klux Klan, and threatening to "whack" Martin Luther King (Brouillette and Randazzo 2009, 91). In the racist Mafia milieu, Marcello could not afford to be seen as a "n----- lover." Brouillette wavers in his assessment of the Little Man's racial attitudes, calling him "hypocritical" before concluding that he "was probably every bit the racist and every bit the hepcat," someone who enjoyed Black culture and associated with Black people yet proclaimed his loathing of them to whites. In this, he was, according to Brouillette, "a pretty good representative of 1950s New Orleans" (92).

Carlos Marcello was the mob boss of New Orleans (and Louisiana), but Gaspar Gulotta was the "Little Mayor of Bourbon Street," as he was popularly known. When he died in 1957, the *New York Times* described the Sicilian-born Gulotta as "a smiling, round little man" who "was always ready to help other bar owners and other French Quarter residents" ("Gaspar Gulotta Is Dead" 1957). Brouillette identifies him as one member of a three-man team that Marcello assembled to run the French Quarter. (The other two were restaurateur "Diamond Jim" Moran—born James Brocato—and bookmaker Sam Saia, the "kingpin of sports betting in the South" [Brouillette and Randazzo 2009, 62].) Gulotta was "the last of the great French Quarter saloon bosses and underworld fixers," the street boss collected bribes for cops and politicians (72). After the deaths of Marcello's three henchmen, the New Orleans Mafia's domination of the French Quarter "was never as complete or as lucrative" (120). Without Gulotta's political savvy and the "decades of piled-up favors to call in," various factions in New Orleans's notoriously corrupt police department, the district attorney's office, and bought-off politicians "got greedy"; police shakedowns, vice squad raids, and "extortionate" indictments by the district attorney ended the mob's so-called golden age in the French Quarter (120–121).

New Orleans Sicilians who remember the French Quarter of the 1950s as a carnivalesque but well-run entertainment district where locals and tourists didn't need to worry about their physical safety (or that of their wallets) often overlook or minimize its unsavory aspects, the racism, corruption, and the dominance of organized crime. The tourists also rarely witnessed the violence that could unpredictably erupt in Bourbon Street and French Quarter venues. Johnny Pennino is a saxophonist who, over a more than seven-decade career, has performed and recorded with dozens of recording artists—New Orleanians like Professor Longhair, Ernie K-Doe, Aaron Neville, and Carlo Ditta, and such national stars as Sam Cooke, Freddy Fender, and Kenny Rogers. "I've done everything from Dixieland, jazz, country, rock 'n' roll, blues, avant-garde, you name it," he says (De Stefano 2017a). Pennino even caught the ear of Duke Ellington, who, on a tip from his trumpeter Cat Anderson, went to hear him play at Papa Joe's on Bourbon Street. Impressed by what he heard, Ellington approached Pennino after his performance to praise his playing.

Notwithstanding a visit by the elegant Ellington, Papa Joe's was far from a *soigné boite*. It was owned by Joe Conforto and operated by him and his three sons. The Confortos, according to our Virgil of the French Quarter Underground, Frenchy Brouillette, were boxers who "liked to drink, raise hell, and beat the shit out of their customers in bar fights" (Brouillette and Randazzo 2009, 62). The Confortos tried to ingratiate themselves with Carlos Marcello, but the closest connection they established with the Little Man was through marriage—Joe Conforto Jr.'s wife was a burlesque entertainer who danced at a bar owned by Marcello's brother Pete. Duke Ellington's visit and praise for Johnny Pennino's playing was a high point of Pennino's days as a Bourbon Street musician. The typical reality was not so glamorous. "Man, if you could have been a fly on the wall at Papa Joe's. The twenty years I put in that place. Let me tell you, it was something else, buddy," Pennino told me in a long, late-night conversation on a park bench at Lake Pontchartrain after he'd played a gig. "They had a guy, his name was Jeremy Sanfilippo. They called him the Hammer Man. You know why? He had a chrome-plated ball-peen hammer in his coat pocket. If a guy give him trouble, bip bip, he put two holes in their head" (De Stefano, 2017a).

Pennino witnessed violent clashes in the French Quarter, including shootings. But he says he was never threatened or harmed because he was protected by a man he calls "my godfather" and "the godfather," Anthony Carolla. Carolla was the son of Silvestro "Silver Dollar Sam" Carolla, a notorious New Orleans mafioso deported to Italy in 1947. Anthony was Carlos Marcello's underboss and successor after Marcello's death in 1993. Pennino recalls Carolla telling him that he had laid down the law to some rough characters in the French Quarter: "He told me he said, you better not let nothing happen to Johnny. Because, if you do, we coming for your fucking ass. Boy, let me tell you, they never let nothing happen to me" (De Stefano 2017a). Carolla was friends with Pennino's father, and after Charles Pennino died when Johnny was in his early twenties, Carolla offered comfort and something more.

"I said, well, Mr. Anthony, I don't have nobody now," Pennino recalled. "He looked at me and says, 'Let me tell you something, son. From this day forward, you have me. I am your godfather. Whatever you want, whatever you need, you come to me.' I hugged him and kissed him on his cheek. He kissed me back on my cheek. He says, 'You the son I never had.' He says, 'I had three siblings and all of them didn't give a shit about me.' He says his son stole a hundred and fifty large [$150,000] from him. Me? I wouldn't take a quarter from that man. That's how much I loved him" (De Stefano 2017a).

That Sicilians owned and operated many businesses on Bourbon Street and in the French Quarter is not disputed. But were these entrepreneurs really mafiosi or even Mafia associates? Frenchy Brouillette and Matt Randazzo certainly make a credible case that they were, and *Mr. New Orleans* is hardly the only book to do so. Johnny Pennino's recollections of his "godfather" Anthony Carolla are certainly not the only Mafia stories New Orleanians told me—mostly off the record. Richard Campanella, however, balks at the claim that the Mafia controlled Bourbon Street and the French Quarter. "I wouldn't use the word 'controlled,'" he said. "'Control' sounds to me like 80, 90 percent: there are these machinations, they're meeting in a room and calling all the shots." Campanella describes the Mafia's presence as "more a behind-the-scenes, influential consortium that coordinated a substantial amount of the really high-profit illegal activity. What is inside and what is outside the Mob? If you make a deal with one of these guys, does that make you an insider? Are you a mobster, then? Or are you just trying to keep your business—here's 100 bucks, keep me safe.' That's why I'm very cautious about this" (De Stefano 2014).

"You'd have bars, some clubs, a restaurant, and something completely unrelated, like an electrical store. And in the backrooms of many bars and clubs, you might have a pinball machine that really was controlled by the Mob. They paid off the bartender to make sure only they got the money. There were these bookmakers and poker machines and illegal gambling. Meanwhile, a legitimate bar was up and running, and the bartenders might have nothing to do with the mobsters. But make no mistake, there were a number of owners who were out and out mobsters" (De Stefano 2014).

Matthew Randazzo isn't persuaded by Campanella's distinctions. While working on *Mr. New Orleans*, he spoke with

> dozens of people from that generation, and I mean not just wiseguys [but also] burlesque dancers, bartenders, pimps and whores and madams, cops. . . . I talked to people of the 1940s and '50s French Quarter. There was no doubt who ran it. The gambling rackets were definitely controlled by the Mob. Jukebox rackets were definitely controlled by the Mob. All the entertainment rackets were definitely controlled by the Mob. The police were controlled by the Mob. A lot of the liquor was controlled by the Mob. So, if I couldn't be in business without doing business with the Mob, did that make me mobbed up? I would suggest, yeah, it does. I suggest that if you were in business four or five different ways with the Mafia in order to be open, then yes, you were mobbed up. Doesn't mean you were a mobster. Doesn't mean you're a mafioso, but it most certainly means you're mobbed up, and I don't think it was possible to be successful in the French Quarter otherwise. I don't know how far back it goes, but I'd probably say at least the '40s and '50s, but I would probably bet also the '30s and '20s. (De Stefano 2018)

Jimmy Anselmo, a retired music promoter and club owner, grew up in the mob-dominated French Quarter of the 1950s and 1960s. He spent his youth on Bourbon Street and in some ways has never left it. Born in Tremé in 1944, Anselmo isn't a musician, but the Louisiana Music Hall of Fame inducted him as a member in 2014 because of his longtime involvement in New Orleans's live music scene. After being discharged from the navy in 1965, he got his first job in the French Quarter as a bartender at Papa Joe's. While serving drinks in the wee hours to the bar's motley clientele of hustlers, strippers, prostitutes, and pimps, Anselmo befriended musicians who eventually would play at his namesake club. One of them was Mac Rebennack, who, before he became famous as Dr. John, would stop by Papa Joe's after playing gigs at other Bourbon Street bars. In 1966, Anselmo opened Co-ed's Tavern on Carrollton Avenue. From 1972 to 1975, he owned and operated Quasimodo's, a music bar popular with university students. Then in 1978 he launched Jimmy's Music Club on Willow Street in the uptown Carrollton neighborhood. The club's first opening act was local favorites Li'l Queenie & the Percolators.

Until it closed in 2000, Jimmy's Music Club presented an eclectic blend of local, national, and international acts. New Orleans eminences like Professor Longhair, Earl King, Dr. John, the virtuoso pianist James Booker, the Meters, and the Neville Brothers played there, as did the legendary bluesmen Muddy Waters and Clarence "Gatemouth" Brown; Bonnie Raitt; reggae stars Burning Spear and Toots and the Maytals; Joan Baez; Iggy Pop; the Red Hot Chili Peppers; A Flock of Seagulls; Asleep at the Wheel, and many others. The club also became the main venue for New Orleans's punk and New Wave scene in the 1980s, presenting such bands as the Cold, Dash Rip Rock, the Sheiks, and the Models. The Cold was led by Vance DeGeneres, a New Orleans native and brother of comedian and talk-show host Ellen DeGeneres.

Jimmy Anselmo was born into the French Quarter's entertainment scene. His father, James Anselmo Sr., known as "Jimmy 'King,'" was a middle-weight boxer from 1922 to 1930. Jimmy told me his father boxed under a pseudonym because "back then, you couldn't be a boxer with an Italian name" (De Stefano 2016b). After his boxing career ended, Jimmy "King" Anselmo Sr. owned and operated several Bourbon Street establishments. He was a handsome man, tall, olive-skinned, with thick, wavy black hair and a trimmed mustache. His son, whose mother Mary Johnson Anselmo was not Sicilian, is shorter and stocky, with bushy white hair, a toothy grin, and a strong accent New Orleanians call "yat" (derived from the greeting, "Where y'at," where you at? i.e., how are you doing?).

On a September afternoon, Jimmy gave me a driving tour of the French Quarter. As he drove through its narrow streets, he pointed out establishments his father had owned or the locations they formerly occupied. Some were places Jimmy frequented as a young man. "Right here on the corner, that was called Madame Francine's. It was a strip club, but later on in the night, they'd have musicians. That's where Dr. John played before he was Dr. John" (De Stefano 2016b).

"When he was Mac Rebennack," I said.

"Right. I'd roam these little streets. I'd love to spend the weekend with my dad because he'd give me a dollar to go to the movie theater, and I got to walk up and down Bourbon and ... I forgot how old I was, but he said, 'Come on in. See my show.' Bought me a Coke. I sat down. That's where I first met Mac" (De Stefano 2016b).

As we approached a building at the corner of Bourbon and Iberville Streets, he pointed to it and said, "Right here, this building was a place called Tony Bacino's. It was a gay club. My dad worked part-time as a bouncer at Tony Bacino's because there were thugs that would come in there and want to beat up on the gays. My dad wore a black glove and had a slapjack. Nobody fought with my dad. My dad was one bad character in New Orleans" (De Stefano 2016b).

"Big guy, I guess," I said.

"Six-foot-two," he said, and then pointed out the window. "Some of the oldest restaurants in America are right over here. He had that place, that place, that place. After the Mardi Gras Lounge, he opened a black nightclub called The Big Hat Lounge. Real quick, this place right over here—my dad had a restaurant called King's Spaghetti House" (De Stefano 2016b).

Jimmy's description of his father as "one bad character" is as close as he will come to acknowledging that he, if not a "made man" in the Mafia, certainly was connected, as he would have had to have been to be a professional boxer in New Orleans and a nightlife entrepreneur on Bourbon Street. The Sicilian expression *in odore di Mafia* seems apt; it covers businesspeople, merchants, lawyers and other professionals, and politicians, who, though not formal members, have the Mafia's "odor," in that they are in its orbit and benefit from their relationships with it.

In 1940, Jimmy "King" Anselmo became a murder suspect after a shooting in a French Quarter saloon. Early in the morning of July 27, he got into an argument with Frank Porretto, an ex-convict and narcotics dealer, and Victor Michel, another thug, at the Cat and the Fiddle, a saloon on Dauphine Street owned by Joe Segreto, a well-known French Quarter figure. The two had been shaking down French Quarter businesses for "protection" money. Although Jimmy is unsure whether they came into Segreto's place to extort its owner, his father and Michel ended up brawling, with Porretto joining the fray. Guns were drawn, and Porretto crawled out of the Cat and the Fiddle with six bullets in him and died in the street. Jimmy "King" and Segreto were arrested and tried for murder; both were acquitted three years later (Karst 2017).

Jimmy Anselmo is retired from the club business; Jimmy's Music Club now is a venue called The Willow. ("Founded in 2014, The Willow is the proverbial Phoenix of Uptown, New Orleans; rising from the ashes of the once-great Jimmy's music club, and we've been keeping the music alive in this historic location ever since.") Two of his close friends, Mac "Dr. John" Rebennack and Art Neville of the Neville Brothers, died in 2019. Other stalwarts of the New Orleans music scene of the 1950s to the 1970s, like former Meters guitarist Leo Nocentelli and singers Aaron Neville and Irma Thomas, are in their seventies and eighties.

Anselmo lives in New Orleans with his wife and their cats. He spends a lot of time on social media, posting photos and articles about his father, the French Quarter, and Jimmy's Music Club. (He created a Facebook page, "I Attended Concerts at Jimmy's Music Club in New Orleans," for former patrons to post their memories of his club.) A committed Democrat, he frequently shares critical articles on Facebook about Donald Trump (he loathes the ex-president) and the

Republican Party. He told me that he has bitter arguments with conservative, Trump-supporting relatives. He finds it hard to comprehend that the descendants of a group that once experienced discrimination and violence could support a president and a party that foment and exploit bigotry.

The colorful, louche, and violent world of Jimmy "King" Anselmo—and of Carlos Marcello, Gaspar Gulotta, Frenchy Brouillette, and countless others who thrived in the mob-dominated French Quarter of the 1950s—is long gone, having ended with the Mafia's demise. After controlling illicit and legitimate business from the 1930s through the 1960s, the New Orleans Mafia began to decline in the 1970s and petered out in the 1980s (Campanella 2014, 242). Organized crime has been replaced by street crime; shootings and other violent assaults plague Bourbon Street, as they do in other parts of New Orleans. (In 2022, New Orleanians disgusted by the city's violent crime began a movement to recall Mayor LaToya Cantrell.) Bourbon Street today is clotted with bars, tacky souvenir shops, and fast-food places. The wonderful music that made New Orleans world famous—jazz, traditional and modern; rhythm and blues; classic rock 'n' roll, funk—is heard mainly on jukeboxes and sound systems. The live music scene shifted years ago to Frenchmen Street in Marigny.

Entertainment venues on Bourbon and Frenchmen Streets annually generate millions in tourism dollars for New Orleans and Louisiana. Yet New Orleans makes it difficult for its musicians to make a living or even live in the city. Successive administrations have failed to meet the urgent and growing need for affordable housing; as the local publication *Gambit* observed, "Long gone are the days of cheap rent in New Orleans" (Ravits 2021). Black musicians in New Orleans today may not be subject to the racist indignities that Deacon John and others have described. But they, and working musicians in general, still face daunting obstacles in a city whose identity—and economy—is inextricably tied to music. Whereas Jim Crow and organized crime once circumscribed the opportunities available to musicians, today, gentrification and soaring rents are pushing them farther and farther from places where they can practice the art that, more than any other, defines New Orleans culture.

Few Sicilian Americans still live in the French Quarter in the twenty-first century, although some still own properties there. The Sicilian presence, once so pervasive, is now mainly evident in the annual St. Joseph's Day celebrations. But in one respect, Bourbon Street hasn't changed. The strip remains the city's biggest tourist attraction, the heart of its entertainment scene, and, to visitors from the United States and beyond, synonymous with New Orleans itself.

## Works Cited

Broom, Sarah M. 2019. *The Yellow House*. New York: Grove.

Brouillette, Frenchy and Matthew V. Randazzo. 2009. *Mr. New Orleans: The Life of a Big Easy Underworld Legend*. Beverly Hills: Phoenix Books.

Campanella, Richard. 2014. *Bourbon Street: A History*. Baton Rouge: Louisiana State University Press.

De Stefano, George. n.d. A review of *Last Call: The Rise and Fall of Prohibition*, by Daniel Okrent. *New York Journal of Books*. https://www.nyjournalofbooks.com/book-review/last-call-rise-and-fall-prohibition.

De Stefano, George. 2014. "The Mafia on Bourbon Street, the Street That New Orleanians Love to Hate." *La Voce di New York*. https://www.lavocedinewyork.com/en/2014/07/08/the-mafia-on-bourbon-street-the-street-that-new-orleanians-love-to-hate-interview-with-richard-campanella-professor-at-tulane-university/.

De Stefano, George. 2016a. Author interview, Jeannine Matranga Ickes.

De Stefano, George. 2016b. Author interview, Jimmy Anselmo.

De Stefano, George. 2017a. Author interview, Johnny Pennino.

De Stefano, George. 2017b. Author interview, Deacon John Moore.

De Stefano. George. 2017c. Author interview, Michael Tessitore.

De Stefano, George. 2018. Author interview, Matthew Randazzo V.

Dr. John (Mac Rebennack) with Jack Rummel. 1994. *Under a Hoodoo Moon: The Life of the Night Tripper*. New York: St. Martin's Griffin.

"Gaspar Gulotta Is Dead." 1957. *New York Times*, December 31, 16.

Hart, Katherine. 2021. "Revival Plans for Dew Drop Inn Move Forward." *Uptown Messenger*. https://uptownmessenger.com/2021/02/revival-plans-for-the-dew-drop-inn-move-forward/.

Jackson, Joy. 1978. "Prohibition in New Orleans: The Unlikeliest Crusade." *Louisiana History: The Journal of the Louisiana Historical Association*, No. 3 (Summer), 269.

Karst, James. 2017, 2019. "Our Times: New Orleans Boxing Legend Becomes a Murder Suspect." *Times-Picayune*. https://www.nola.com/entertainment_life/vintage/article_3a768165-b4d6-5875.

Ravits, Sarah. 2021. "Model Homes: Sixteen Years On It's Time to Learn Lessons from Post-Katrina Housing Initiatives." *Gambit*. https://www.nola.com/gambit/news/the_latest/model-homes-sixteen-years-on-it-s-time-to-learn-lessons-from-post-katrina-housing/article_1933016c-0125-11ec-9e9e-af5e3c891a37.html.https://www.thewillowuptown.com/about-us.

Souther, Mark J. 2006. *New Orleans on Parade: Tourism and the Transformation of the Crescent City*. Baton Rouge: Louisiana State University Press.

Suhor, Charles. 2001. *Jazz in New Orleans: The Postwar Years Through 1970*. Lanham, MD: Scarecrow Press.

Walker, David. "Take a tour of Bourbon Street's music scene of the 1950s." 2020. The Historic New Orleans Collection. https://www.hnoc.org/publications/first-draft/take-tour-bourbon-streets-music-scene-1950s#:~:text=Segregation%20was%20in%20full%20force,the%20street%20itself%20without%20harassment.

# Spike Lee's Colliding Images of the Antagonistic and Loving Relationships Between African Americans and Italian Americans in *Jungle Fever*

MARK A. REID

When considering the interethnic value of Spike Lee's *Jungle Fever* (1991), one cannot avoid the intertextual social history that the film and Roberto Rossellini's *Paisan* (*Paisà*) (1946) both express. These values show transracial and transnational humanistic principles. This paper explores some cinematic elements, including cinematographic style, auditory elements, and mise-en-scène configurations, that contribute to a bid for compassion during internecine historical moments when war and social chaos rule society. Such examples of the conflict territories can be found in both Lee's movie and in the neo-realist *Paisan*, which features a WWII African American soldier who cares for an orphaned child in the film's second episode on Napoli.

Lee's *Jungle Fever* reflects a similar transracial caring by its complex unpacking of the psychology that enabled the murder of Yusuf K. Hawkins that took place in New York City in the Bensonhurst neighborhood in 1989. Lee's film is a poetic refiguration of the incident by othering a few Italian Americans as altruistic mediators who become outliers in their public and domestic spaces within Bensonhurst, Brooklyn, a predominantly Italian American working-class neighborhood. *Jungle Fever* explores complex Italian American characters, including young neighborhood men like those who could have participated in the murder of Yusuf Hawkins.

The second episode of Rossellini's *Paisan* features Joe, a Black WWII MP who meets and shows compassion for Pasquale, a homeless Italian child who steals his boots. (See figure 1.) *Jungle Fever* and *Paisan* evince similar humanistic messages during the internecine historical moments of a world war and racist mob violence.

Rossellini employs strategic narrative maneuvers to show Joe's humanity; using similar cinematic devices, Lee allows a few Italian American characters—Paulie, Angie, and Denise—a transracial humanity of heroic proportions. Their scenes are balanced against characters with different degrees of racism and sexism.

*Jungle Fever* employs parallel stylistic borrowings that relate to contemporary events and Italian American culture—singers like Frank Sinatra and culturally effective mise-en-scène images as visual and auditory references to local politicians, sports, and entertainment figures. For instance, Lee includes music from three Frank Sinatra recordings: "Hello, Young Lovers" (written by Richard Rogers and Oscar Hammerstein II), "It Was a Very Good Year" (written and scored by Ervin Drake), and "Once Upon a Time" (lyrics by Lee Adams, music by Charles Strouse). These songs embellish scenes with auditory elements of the antagonistic and loving relationships between African Americans and Italian Americans.

Lee's cinematographic depictions of racial, gendered, and sexual internecine challenges are exploratory rather than definitive since spectators observe cruel characters that Paulie, Angie, and Denise question and propose benevolent actions and words. Lee situates his major protagonists in their familiar ethnic surroundings such as their homes, places of work, and neighborhood hangouts. These settings are fertile for transethnic antagonism, romantic love, and friendship. In such settings where family, friends, and policing agents interact, *Jungle Fever* explores the internecine elements that define contemporary American life. Two Black female characters, Orin and Inez, and two Italian American characters, Paulie and Angie, resist being pulled into conflict. With these characters, Lee offers intervention stratagems and avoids the very racism, bigotry, and misogyny that certain film critics accused him of promoting in his films. Contrary to such criticisms, *Jungle Fever,* and *Do the Right Thing* (1989) develop and dramatize ethnic conflict themes and explore them dialogically through the characters (most notably the pizzeria owner Sal in *Do the Right Thing*).

*Jungle Fever* features fertile sociopsychological situations where transethnic antagonism, romantic love, and friendship overlap to reveal America's interethnic failures that make outliers of their own community members. The Black characters Orin and Inez, and the white characters Angie, Paulie, and Denise are the only ones who avoid hurtful reactions to transracial socializing whether platonic or sexual in form. These characters resist their community's everyday acts of racism, bigotry, and misogyny. In various ways, they strategically deconstruct the language and practices of violent bigotry and sexism, which are mutually destructive to the city and the nation.

RACE, ETHNICITY, CLASS, AND GENDER HIERARCHIES: A MOMENTARY, LOVING, CONTENTIOUS, AND ADULTEROUS INTERRACIAL AFFAIR

Most of *Jungle Fever*'s characters unwittingly or knowingly take part in acts of racism and misogyny. Flipper Purify and Angie's two brothers are notable members of this chauvinist group. Later in the film, Vinny directs the mob against the Italian American character Paulie, and Mike beats his daughter Angie. These violent acts are in response to Angie's interracial intimacy with a Black man and Paulie's date with a Black woman. Contrastingly, Flipper's racial and sexual chauvinism lies in his psychological abuse of his Black wife Drew and his white lover Angie. Unlike Flipper, Drew and Angie are sincere in their love and concern for him. (See figures 2–5.)

One late evening, Angie summons her two girlfriends Denise and Louise for a meeting in the neighborhood park, during which she reveals that she is dating a Black guy from work. Angie seeks their support and guidance. Both provide different suggestions and viewpoints about interracial dating. Denise approves with caution due to the recent murder of an African American teenager (Yusuf Hawkins) who entered their neighborhood. Louise is appalled, saying, "Personally, I think it's disgusting. . . . Yeah, I think it's gross. How could you? . . . Me, myself, personally, I could never." (See figure 6.) Denise is nonjudgmental and responds, "You're not sleeping with the guy. What do you care? This is the Nineties. There's nothing wrong with it. You having a good time?" Their dialogue, reflections, and eventual support reveal a more lenient attitude than that of the men in their lives. Still, neither of her two friends would accept a transracial romance for themselves, as the following dialogue demonstrates.

Denise: What's so important? I'm to go out with Vinny. What'd you get us here
    for? What's going on?
Louise: You gonna finally have a wedding?
Angie: No... I don't know.
Denise: But you're wearing that ring.
Louise: Why do you look so happy?
Denise: So, what is it?
Louise: What's going on?
Angie: But you gotta swear. This is like swearing on Bibles. Swearing on rosary
    beads.
Denise: I swear on my great grandmother, okay? We swear, we swear, what?
Angie: I'm seeing somebody.
Denise: ...you two-timing?
Louise: Who are you seeing?
Angie: Somebody from work.
Louise: So, what's he look like? Who is this guy?
Denise: What's his name?

Angie: Flipper.

Denise: And what is he? Blond, blue-eyed surfer type?

Angie: He's Black. Something wrong with your face?

Denise: Black? You did it with a Black guy?

Angie: Yeah.

Denise: If your father ever found out. I don't know.

Angie: He's not gonna . . .

Angie: I'm just saying keep it quiet.

Denise: Look at Gina.

Angie: Gina who?

Denise: She brought that guy into the neighborhood, that Black guy. Look what they did to him.

Louise: What you talking about that Puerto Rican crackhead for?

Denise: She brought him into the neighborhood, and they killed the guy. You better be careful.

Louise: I don't think she's stupid enough to bring him in.

Denise: Whatever. Our lips are sealed.

Inez is Drew's friend and the only person who expresses an openness to interracial dating. The issue of interracial romance comes up when a group of African American women gather to console Drew after Flipper pursues an adulterous affair with Angie. Inez's affirmative response to interracial intimacy deviates from the guiding opinion on interracial intimacy that the other Black women keep. However, Drew states that her hurt lies in Flipper's adultery; the woman's ethnicity does not matter. *Jungle Fever*'s most open-minded characters are two Black women, Inez and Orin, and two white female characters, Angie and Denise, who share similar views on interracial and interethnic dating. (See figure 7.)

For example, Inez states, "I do date Black men; but I also date Chinese, Latino, Jewish . . . the full spectrum." She adds, "You think I should date Black men, but I'm gonna date who I like. Give me a man, regardless of color, who is nice to me, sweet to me, and who I believe loves me." Considering interracial romance, Inez's response stands out. In varying degrees, the other women in Drew's Black sisterhood circle seem to share Louise's opinion on this subject. Still, none of these Black and white women who oppose interracial intimacy express their feeling with threats of violence and religious condemnation. Physical and psychological violence are the tools used by Vinny, Frankie Botz, Patty, Veeshay, and Sonny, the men who congregate in Paulie's place of business, his father's candy store. The Good Reverend Purify, father of Flipper and Gator, shares in the racial bigotry. *Jungle Fever* transforms the bombastic character Radio Raheem in Lee's *Do the Right Thing* into Flipper Purify, the talented, self-centered architect.

In contrast to Lashawn and most other Black female characters in *Jungle Fever*, Orin recommends that Paulie enroll in college and supplies him an application and a course catalogue. She offers Paulie antiracist intervention methods that contest, resist, and avoid the racism, bigotry, classicism, and misogyny that most of the characters exhibit.

Flipper takes Angie to the Harlem restaurant Sylvia's, where a hostile Lashawn is their server. The exchange between Flipper and Lashawn underlines the antagonism that the interracial couple encounters from friends and family in the public spaces they encounter throughout the film. (See figure 8.)

In a verbal exchange with Flipper, Lashawn is confrontational, and her aversion to Flipper and Angie as a couple recalls the earlier scenes in which Vinny bullies Paulie. Lashawn is not a rabid racist as are the men that meet at Lou Carbone's candy store. Nonetheless, she expresses her disdain for interracial dating. This is Flipper's first opportunity to resist. This heated and demeaning exchange of words is the first of three racist encounters that the couple endures. If survival and love conquer the whirlwind of hate, the film's narrative would enable a shared resistance strategy that would support their adulterous interracial union. *Jungle Fever* shines a light on ordinary racism, toxic masculinity, and their omniscient presence in society.

The Purify elders, their son Flipper, and Angie make up a unique family characterized by love and antagonism. The Sylvia's restaurant scene in Harlem prompted Flipper's first reality check about the quality of reception for transracial dating in the Black public sphere. The public racism at Sylvia's is followed by a domesticated version. At dinner at the Good Reverend and Lucinda Purify's home, Reverend Purify cites biblical passages to shame the interracial couple. It is in this context that Flipper and Angie receive their second Afrocentric warning when Reverend Purify delivers his sermon on miscegenation, which is received with evident misery by Lucinda, Flipper, and Angie. Still, the two events are not the last ones that directly involve Flipper's meeting with the racist formation of the internecine within public and familial spaces. (See figure 9.)

> Rev. Purify: White man says to his woman: "Baby, you are the flower of white Southern womanhood, too holy and pure to be touched by any man, including me. I'm gonna put you up on a pedestal so the whole world will fall down and worship you. And if any nigger so much as look at you, I'll lynch his ass."

The Good Reverend Purify continues to shame Flipper and Angie with insensitive and racist conjecture.

> But in the midnight hour, layin' there, alone, on the hot bed of lust, I'm sure they must've thought what it would be like to have one of them big, Black bucks their husbands were so desperately afraid of. I feel sorry for you. Here it is the nineties, still tryin' to make up for what you missed out on. But I don't blame you. As for the Black man like my own son, Flipper, who ought to know better got a loving wife and daughter still got to fish in the white man's cesspool, I have nothing but contempt. Excuse me. I don't eat with whoremongers.

This heated and demeaning familial exchange differs from the public sphere of normalized racist encounters with policing apparatuses that check those public spaces. The film depicts Flipper and Angie as the racialized *other(ed)* couple. Fortunately, such a transracial union does develop between Paulie Carbone and Orin Goode. However, this does not occur with Flipper and Angie's adulterous affair because their romance transgresses religious principles and public jurisprudence.

When Flipper parks his car on the street of their West Village apartment, he and Angie goof around pretend-boxing as they mention the names of renowned figures in the boxing world, including manager and trainer Constantine "Cus" D'Amato, who managed and trained world heavyweight champion boxers Mike Tyson, Floyd Patterson, and José Torres. The police arrive with their guns drawn on Flipper because a neighbor had reported that a Black male was assaulting a Caucasian woman. Ironically, the two had just escaped his home and the untouched dinner that his mother prepared. (See figure 10.)

> Officer Long: Get your hands up! Put 'em up. Put 'em up. Get your hands up! Get your hands up.
> Flipper: What'd I do?
> Officer Long: Against the wall!
> Officer Sandoval: You all right, ma'am?
> Angie: I'm all right. Let go of me. That's my boyfriend. What are you doing?
> Officer Sandoval: Get back.
> Flipper: I'm not her boyfriend. We're just lovers ... just friends.
> Angie: This must be some kind of mistake.
> Flipper: Angie, shut up. She doesn't know what she's talkin' about.
> Officer Long: He wasn't trying to rape you?
> Angie: No!

Flipper: I didn't do anything.

Angie: Take the gun from his head.

Officer Long: Talk to me. What?

Flipper: It's just a big misunderstanding. That's all.

Officer Long: Slow. Turn around.

Flipper: I was just makin' sure she got home safe.

Officer Long: All right. Sorry about that. No harm, no foul.

Officer Sandoval: We got a call that an Afro-American male was attacking a Caucasian woman.

Officer Long: You all right, man? Just a little excitement.

Flipper: No problem.

Officer Long: What? Give me a reason, man!

Angie: Don't you dare try it! Are you crazy? I'll have your badge. I'll bring you up on charges!

Flipper: Shut up. Shut up.

Angie: I'm gonna report this.

Flipper: What's the matter with you telling 'em we're lovers! You tryin' to get me killed.

Angie: It's none of their business.

Flipper: What a waste! What the fuck am I doin' here?


Flipper's three different unwanted encounters with Black public and private moments of racist confrontation take place at different demographic points in New York City—Harlem and Greenwich Village. The conglomeration of racism leads to Flipper's capitulation. He ignores Angie's loving protestations and fearless attitude toward the police officers. Flipper offers Angie the beating, though psychological, that her father Mike (physically) and the Good Reverend Purify (morally) dealt Angie, berating her for IDing him as her lover.

When Mike Tucci discovers that Angie, his daughter, is dating a Black man, he insults Angie and violently slaps and beats her until her brothers, Charlie and Jimmy, restrain him. This violent, misogynist scene is aurally infused with Mike's shouts of "Nigger lover!" A similar violent patriarchal outburst occurs as the film end, which involves Lou, Paulie's father, and later the men that frequent the candy store. The men knock Paulie to the ground and conitinue their group punishment. Paulie rises and continues on his path to make his date with Orin. (See figure 11.)

Paulie informs his father that he is going on a date. His father is momentarily relieved until he discovers that Paulie's date is with a Black woman. The two men have a heated argument over race, the burdens of managing Lou's candy store, and the motherless Carbone home. Their exchange and Paulie's response are determined. Lou inquires, "A date. Who with?" and Paulie says that his date is with Orin Good. His father's immediate response is "She's . . . She's . . . She's black. You don't bring no brown sugar home to this house! If your mother was alive, she'd turn over in her grave! You are not my son! You bastard. Fuckin' . . . You are not my son! You bastard! You are not my son."

Both fathers react violently when they discover that their children are dating African Americans. These unfatherly outbursts of rage overflow into the streets of the Carbone and Tucci homes and go on to involve the candy store patrons. When Paulie reponds to their queries about his date this night, they respond by attacking him, and Paulie smashes Vinny's head against a metal garbage bin. Vinny asks "You goin' out with that fuckin' nigger? You think you're better than me, Paulie? You're a fuckin' disgrace. Asshole, you're no better than me . . . Fuckin' piece of shit, Paulie." Vinny's words ignite all the candy store freeloaders who join in the beating. But Paulie's determination leads him, bloodied, to Orin's front door where she welcomes him. He has navigated the boundaries of race, toxic masculinity, and their imagined and intolerant parental and fraternal communities to meet his date.

Previously, Paulie had been a reflective, passive guy whose strengths lay in his compassion, egalitarian attitude, and his intersectional antiracist take on African American and the Italian American sociocultural experience. Paulie's and Vinny's heated verbal exchanges indicate their opposing viewpoint on racial matters, as when Paulie discussed the racial lynching of eleven Italians in New Orleans that resulted from an Italian American factory owner who hired African American workers.

Paulie, Angie, and, in a smaller way key, Angie's friend Denise resist and interrogate the dominant male discourse that is found in both Black and white ethnic communities. Denise supports Angie's freedom of romantic choice and acknowleges that times are changing. Ironically, Denise's boyfriend Vinny is the film's most rabid racist and misogynist.

Lou and Mike's reactions reflect similar violent inclinations that produce physical and psychological harm to their young adult children. In a parallel but lethal manner, the Good Reverend Doctor Purify shoots his drug-addicted son Gator. I suspect that the Good Reverend shares the same fears held and acted upon as his Italian American bretheren. His faith is grounded in that same fear that underlies racial bigotry. Like Flipper, the Reverend is unwilling and unable to get past a kind of loveless state of limbo where the sincerity of Angie's love is mistaken for lust.

It is important to understand how this film offers an alternative to monolithic images of good and bad New York City communities where racist mobs exist. *Jungle Fever* problematizes one-dimensional receptions in which one racial or ethnic group is demonized because of their class, race, gender, or skin pigment as occurs when Frankie Botz, a candy store regular, is racially othered by Vinny though both are Italian Americans. Lee offers the characters of Angie and Paulie, who question bigotry and racism by resisting their racist and sexist friends and family. In so doing, Lee humanizes the ethnic internecine trope in *Jungle Fever*.

When navigating the boundaries of race, toxic masculinity, and their imagined and intolerant familial communities, Paulie must counter the sexism that Vinny interweaves with his racist thoughts. Additionally, Paulie must confront other men that share Vinny's racism and ethnic chauvinism. Unfortunately, the young men that congregate in the candy store share Vinny's imperfect sensibilities about women and African Americans. Paulie strategically uses Italian American history as a critical device to resist Vinny's everyday racism. He engages Vinny in a fierce exchange over the racial implications of the lynching of the eleven Italian Americans over the hiring of African American workers. Vinny becomes bothered and perplexed by Paulie's constant newspaper reading. Paulie responds with the episode of Italian American history that invokes a transethnic intersectional experience and criticizes an injustice conducted on eleven Italian American men. To persuade Vinny to reconsider his racist views, Paulie attempts to share this information. Vinny retorts, "Good, they got what they deserved. They shouldn't have got involved with no niggers" (Guglielmo 2003; Staples 2019; 1891 New Orleans lynchings 2023)

This scene bridges two historical moments when racial injustice leads to the deaths of innocent citizens: the murderous mob that killed eleven Italian Americans in 1891 New Orleans, and the mob that chased and beat African American teenagers and murdered Yusuf K. Hawkins in 1989 in New York City's Bensonhurst neighborhood. The dialogue between the Italian American characters, the screenplay by Spike Lee, and the collaboration with Lee's actors and American history memorialize the victims of two *racialized* lynchings. In a different cinematographic style, Rossellini's collaboration with Klaus Mann in the episode of *Paisan* of the African American soldier caring for a homeless Italian child expresses similar noble purposes for post–World War II international relations.

When, on August 23, 1989, thirty white youths chased Yusuf K. Hawkins, a sixteen-year-old African American, through Bensonhurst, an Italian American working-class Brooklyn neighborhood, Hawkins was shot dead. "A bitter racial hatred permeated the atmosphere" one writer wrote at the time. "Blacks know what neighborhood they belong to, and we know what neighborhood we belong to," a twenty-three-year-old "100% Italian" explained to a *Los Angeles Times* reporter. "It comes down to boundary lines. You're always going to have racism wherever you go" (Krajicek 2019).

Gina Feliciano and Yusuf Hawkins had never met, yet Bensonhurst teenage males organized a racist mob to attack Yusuf and his Black male friends who had gone with him to the neighborhood where he planned to buy a used car. Gina had broken off a romantic relationship with the young man who organized the mob of baseball-bat and a gun-toting avenging angels. One youth in the mob murdered Yusuf, youths in this same mob beat his friends with bats, and Gina, a Puerto Rican girl, suffered a shaming in all its toxic masculinist colors.

The cinematic worlds reflected in these two films are filled with conflict and misunderstanding, and yet they offer faintly hopeful visions for better futures. Spike Lee's film and its vision are more complex and fragile than Rossellini's, the wound of Hawkins's death being so fresh. But historical knowledge and compassion provide the key to both filmmakers trying to get to the bottom of violence and racial confrontation.

Figure 1. Joe (Dots M Johnson) and Pasquale (Alfonsino Bovino), *Paisà*, episode 2.

Figure 2. Ming Purify (Veronica Timbers), Drew Purify (Lonette McKee), and Flipper Purify (Wesley Snipes), *Jungle Fever*.

Figure 3. Charlie Tucci (David Dundara), Angie Tucci (Annabella Sciorra), Mike Tucci (Frank Vincent), and James Tucci (Michael Imperioli).

Figure 4. Lucinda Purify (Ruby Dee), the Good Reverend Doctor Purify (Ossie Davis), and Flipper.

Figure 5. Angie, Leslie (Brad Dourif),
Flipper, and Jerry (Tim Robbins).

Figure 6. Denise (Debi Mazar) and
Louise (Gina Mastrogiacomo).

Figure 7. Inez (Theresa Randle),
Nilda (Phyllis Yvonne Stickney), and Drew.

Figure 8. Lashawn (Queen Latifa),
Angie, and Flipper.

Figure 9. Lucinda, the Good Reverend Doctor,
Flipper, and Angie.

Figure 10. Flipper and Officer Long (Rick Aiello).

Figure 11. Paulie Carbone (John Turturro)
and Orin Goode (Tyra Ferrell).

## Works Cited

"1891 New Orleans Lynchings." 2022. wikipedia.org/wiki/March_14%2C_1891_New_Orleans_lynchings.

Guglielmo, Jennifer. 2003. "White Lies Dark Truths." In *Are Italians White? How Race Is Made in America*, edited by Jennifer Guglielmo and Salvatore Salerno, 1–14. New York: Routledge. eBook published August 13, 2003.

Krajicek, David J. 2019. "Bigotry in Bensonhurst and the murder of Yusuf Hawkins." *New York Daily News*, July 28, 2019. Accessed February 23, 2023.

Lee, Spike. 1989. *Do the Right Thing*. Universal Pictures. DVD.

Lee, Spike. 1991. *Jungle Fever*. Universal Pictures. DVD.

Rossellini, Roberto. 1946. *Paisan (Paisà)*. Metro-Goldwyn-Mayer. https://www.youtube.com/watch?v= TpYvZyLXag0.

Sciorra, Joseph. 2003. "The Murder of Yusuf Hawkins (R. I. P.) and My March on Bensonhurst." In *Are Italians White? How Race is Made in America*, edited by Jennifer Guglielmo and Salvatore Salerno, 192–209. New York: Routledge. eBook published August 13, 2003. Accessed March 6, 2023.

Staples, Brent. n.d. "How Italians Became 'White.'" https://www.nytimes.com/interactive/2019/10/12/opinion/ columbus-day-italian-american-racism.html9. Accessed July 10, 2022.

United States Holocaust Memorial Museum. n.d. "Klaus Mann Holocaust Encyclopedia." *Holocaust Encyclopedia*. https://encyclopedia.ushmm.org/content/en/article/klaus-mann. Accessed March 15, 2023.

# "Citizens Plead Necessity for White Supremacy" and "Electoral Freaks & Monstrosities": The Racial Transiency of Dixie's Italians in Jim Crow Louisiana[1]

JESSICA BARBATA JACKSON

After five Sicilians were lynched in Tallulah, Louisiana, in July of 1899, the *Times Democrat* of New Orleans published an article in defense of the lynching: "Citizens Plead Necessity for White Supremacy" (1899c). Just the year before, however, as Louisiana legislators disenfranchised Black voters through the implementation of a literacy and property requirement for voting, they also passed a provision—subsequently dubbed the "Privileged Dago" clause—that specifically protected the "foreign white vote" and Italian voting rights. How could Sicilians and other Italians be considered both foreign "white" voters but also be susceptible to lynching? How could Italians fall both outside white supremacy's understanding of whiteness and also within it? And ultimately, what does a close reading of these moments demonstrate about the fluctuating racial categorization of Italian immigrants in turn-of-the-century Louisiana?

Bringing the immigrant narrative into the racially fluid environment and contextual nuance of Louisiana both requires a reconsideration of existing critical whiteness scholarship and reveals that the racial categorization of Italian immigrants in Louisiana at the turn of the century remained variable and unstable. As a result, Louisiana's English-language presses, employing the power and language of race, shaped and informed how an immigrant community could be read (both figuratively and literally). As evidence of the fluidity of Italian racialization—often an aftereffect of violence and disenfranchisement efforts rather than its cause—the language of race could be used to manipulate who had access to citizenship and belonging in 1890s Louisiana.

First, a note on race: critical whiteness scholars have provided a much-needed discourse to understand the intermediary racial status of arriving European immigrants at the end of the nineteenth century (Arnesen 2001; Brodkin 1998; Fields 2001; Guterl 2001; Hale 1999; Harris 1993; Jacobson 1996; Roediger 2005, 2007). James Barrett and David Roediger (1997) consider Eastern and Southern Europeans to be an "inbetween" people, meaning that Italians resided somewhere "inbetween" white and Black.[2] Thomas Guglielmo (2003) counters this characterization of "inbe-tweenness" by suggesting that Italians were "White on Arrival"; Guglielmo explains that although Italians were racially suspect, their whiteness protected them from legal discrimination. Yet how does this determination of Italians as unequivocally white account for the fact that even Italian legal whiteness was not always so secure within the complicated and fluid racial structure of Louisiana?

Rather, the multifaceted racial structure and historical contingency of Louisiana requires a more nuanced and fluid, more fluctuating, and more shifting concept for Italians' racial status than scholars have previously adopted. I provide a new framework for understanding the liminal racial status of Sicilians and other Italians in the US South: racial transiency. This transiency, which highlights the instability of their racialization, meant that Sicilians and other Italians passed among and between racial communities; they moved (and were moved) as both "white southerners" and "people of color" back and forth across the color line. Owing to this racial flexibility, Italians were lynched in defense of white supremacy but could also possess "unconquerable white blood" (*Times Democrat* 1899c; *Columbus Dispatch* 1907). Italians were depicted as contributors and "proper citizens" before the 1891 lynching in New Orleans, but then, in defense of their bloodshed, they were called a "menac[ing] . . . gang of murderers" and "degenerate monsters" (*Times Democrat* 1898a; *Daily Picayune* 1898a, 1898b; *Daily States* 1899a, 1899b). When they marched in the streets to protest disenfranchisement in the 1890s, they were "ignorant [and] brutal" and "a disgrace to a civilized community" but nonetheless granted voting rights as "faithful allies," "good citizens" and "foreign whites" (*Daily Picayune* 1889, 1895,1896a. 1896b; *Biloxi Daily Herald* 1907; *Weekly Messenger* 1891).

To illustrate this concept of racial transiency, I juxtapose two moments in 1890s Louisiana: one that examines the lynching of five Sicilians in 1899 Tallulah and another that considers the political experience of Sicilians and other Italians during the state's 1896–1898 suffrage debates (see Figure 1). Of note, the infamous lynching of eleven Italians in 1891 New Orleans was not the only lynching of Sicilians and other Italians in the Gulf South during the late nineteenth and early twentieth centuries. In fact, more than two dozen Sicilians and other Italians were lynched in the region between 1886 and 1910. In 1899 Madison Parish, Louisiana, trouble began over a goat.

The popular and vivacious Difatta brothers owned two grocery stores in Tallulah: because of their financial success, certain members of the community "regarded [them] with secret animosity," but otherwise, they often caroused with prominent community members, drinking and playing cards (*Papers Relating to the Foreign Relations of the United States* 1899, 445) (see Figure 2). Wednesday, July 19, 1899, began like any other day. In the humid midday heat, a goat belonging to Francesco Difatta wandered onto the property of Dr. J. Ford Hodge. It was not the first occasion that Difatta's goats had trespassed on Hodge's estate. But, having grown impatient from the repeated intrusion, on this particularly sweltering day Hodge drew his revolver and shot the interloping goat. The following day, Francesco, aggrieved for his goat, called to Hodge across his property; they quarreled, exchanging a barrage of animated words, but with "no serious consequences." Francesco Difatta's brother Carlo, less willing to dismiss the incident so easily, upon encountering Hodge later that day, "spoke harshly" with him. As the conversation grew increasingly heated, Carlo struck the doctor with his fist. Although Carlo was otherwise unarmed, Hodge drew and fired his revolver, grazing Carlo on the forehead; as Carlo collapsed, Hodge placed his boot on the fallen Difatta's chest, holding him to the ground. Giuseppe, the third Difatta brother, witnessed the fray from the raised porch of their home. While Hodge worked to clear the chamber of his jammed revolver, boot still firmly planted on Carlo's chest, Giuseppe fired upon Hodge from the balcony with a pistol loaded with birdshot. Word spread swiftly through Madison Parish that "the Italians had killed Dr. Hodge," and the three Difatta brothers were hastily arrested (*Papers Relating to the Foreign Relations of the United States* 1899, 445). The sheriff rounded up Giovanni Cerami and Rosario Fiducia, two Sicilian friends supposedly in cahoots with the "cold-blooded foreigners," on charges of conspiracy (*Times Democrat* 1899a).

Within hours, hysteria over Hodge's shooting enveloped the parish. Disquieting murmurs and anxious broadcasts reported that in an act of premeditated homicide, the Italians had shot Hodge fifty to seventy-five times (*Arkansas Gazette* 1899). With the five Sicilians confined in the parish jail, a crowd "intoxicated with blood" multiplied outside (*Papers Relating to the Foreign Relations of the United States* 1899, 445). After constructing, at a nearby abattoir, a makeshift gallows from a device used to hoist dead cattle for skinning, the throng stormed the parish jail. The mob, reportedly made up of "every able-bodied man in Tallulah," first set their sights on Carlo and Giuseppe, whom they dragged out and marched across the field from the jail to the slaughterhouse; the self-made executioners quickly hanged the two "principal perpetrators" from the jury-rigged scaffold. "There was a rest of some little time" before the crowd turned their attention to Francesco and Rosario, whom they hauled to the front yard of the jailhouse (*Times Democrat* 1899c). With a cigar in his mouth, Francesco called out, "I liva here sixa year . . . I knowa you all—you alla my friends," his final words abruptly cut short as the mob winched the two men from the yard's dominating cottonwood tree (*Times Democrat* 1899c). An hour passed before the dwindling throng returned for Giovanni and likewise pulled him from his cell to be hanged alongside Francesco and Rosario in the jailhouse yard. In three separate acts, the frenzied mob lynched five Sicilians to enact "vengeance upon the guilty" and to "teach the Italian and his gang a lesson" (*Weekly Messenger*

1899). Inhabitants went on to issue a pronouncement warning that "all others of the [Italian] race within the parish lines had three days to leave under penalty of death," at which point the one remaining Sicilian reportedly fled Tallulah (*Times Democrat* 1899b); newspaper reports went on to declare that Tallulah had "emptied their town of Italians" (*Times Democrat* 1899b). Meanwhile, Dr. Hodge survived the shooting and was declared "out of all danger" three days later (*Times Democrat* 1899b).

In the aftermath of the killings, despite the fact that members of the lynch mob were well known in the community, and two "Negro brothers" who witnessed the lynching even provided a list of names to the Italian diplomatic investigators, the Madison Parish Grand Jury concluded that they were "wholly unable to discover the names of the perpetrators of the lynching" (*Notes from the Italian Legation* 1900; *Notes from the Italian Legation* 1899a). The *Times* went on to explain that of the "several lynchings" in Madison Parish in the previous eighteen months, "the result is that Madison Parish is never the scene now of any race troubles. The negroes have come to the realization of the fact that lawlessness on their part will not be tolerated" (*Times Democrat* 1899c).

As to the rationale for the Difattas' executions, previous explanations have suggested that "white" men were lynched because of their lack of "social embeddedness" and because of a particular "outsider" status (Bailey and Tolnay 2015, 192). And yet the Difatta brothers enjoyed a marked degree of social embeddedness within the region. They were popular members of the community who frequently socialized with their native-born, white neighbors; the Difattas had lived in the area for at least six years, while Dr. Hodge had resided in Madison Parish for only a year and a half (*Times Democrat* 1898j, 1898k, 1898l). Diplomatic correspondence noted, "Nothing could be said against [the Difattas]; they never had difficulty with anyone . . . the behavior of these men had always been good" (*Notes from the Italian Legation* 1899b).

Nonetheless, the Difatta brothers' successful grocery business, economic mobility, and commercial success marked them as potential threats to some members of the Tallulah community. In an effort to justify the lynching, select testimonies found ways to portray the Difattas as disreputable residents. Certain press reports went on to describe the brothers as having "fierce and quarrelsome dispositions" and "bad reputations"; they were "violent men, easily excited—thrown into a perfect furry [*sic*] at the least cause," with "no love lost between them and the other inhabitants of the place" (*Daily Picayune* 1899; *Daily States* 1899c; *Times Democrat* 1899d). As Sicilians, they had overstepped their economic place; in so doing, the local native-born, white community read the Difattas' actions—more legally recognizable as self-defense—as criminal and disregarded their right to defend themselves.

Significantly, in the aftermath of the violence, community members and the English-language press strove to defend the killings in racial terms. The language of race was used to validate violence, even if race was only tangentially related to the conditions that instigated the killing. The press protested that "the same punishment would have been vented upon any set of men, no matter whether they were Italians, Englishmen, Germans or natives of the United States" (*Times Democrat* 1899c) but ultimately justified the lynching in explicitly racial terms. The *Times Democrat* titled its piece "Citizens Plead Necessity for White Supremacy" (1899c), indicating that the lynchings upheld "white supremacy." The native-born, white community in Tallulah felt "obliged" to commit the lynchings, since the "complicity in the conspiracy . . . could never have been proven legally, and that to insure [*sic*] white supremacy, no other course was possible than the course pursued" (*Times Democrat* 1899c).

Furthermore, the explicit awareness that the lynchings of these five Sicilians contributed to a culture of fear and coerced compliance from the "negro" community functioned to reduce Italians to the position of nonwhites. Suggesting that "white supremacy" would otherwise be in jeopardy—and identifying the reasons for the murders of these five Sicilians as comparable with the motives behind the killings of African Americans—indicates that Italians could be, when necessary, consigned outside a larger category of whiteness. Relegating Italians to a position outside of "whiteness," which confirmed their racial transiency, presented a popular means to validate the lynching and to ensure the legitimacy of violence that would otherwise undermine white and nativist respectability. Ultimately, this process of racializing Italians was an aftereffect of the violence, rather than its cause.

Native-born, white Louisianians did not lynch Italians because they were Italian, but Italian-ness, read and applied in racial terms, avowed that they were susceptible to being lynched. Their Italianness meant that they could be lynched even while the particularities of these violent episodes resulted from a continuity of causes and specific time and place contextual factors (Luconi 2013, 58; Webb 2008, 178 and 187). Race and ethnicity offered the means to prescribe an outsider status upon Sicilians and other Italians, thus designating them (and perceiving them) as unembedded or foreign even when they were not. The racialized and abjectly anti-Italian discourse in the aftermath of each lynching operated racially and functioned as a discursive means to legitimize the violence. Foremost, if race was not the cause of the Louisiana vigilante violence, the lynchings of Sicilians and other Italians contested their unqualified whiteness and drew into question Italian access to the protections of whiteness in a region governed by white supremacy.

The 1896–1898 disenfranchisement debates similarly revealed not only the racial transiency of Italians but also how the manipulation of racial language played out in discourses on voting. In 1896 Louisiana Democrats proposed a suffrage amendment carefully and explicitly calculated to disenfranchise the state's Black population as well as "illiterate voters," foreigners, and immigrants, and—a major category of contention in Louisiana—"declarant aliens" (noncitizen immigrants who had made known their intention to naturalize). Louisiana's declarant alien clause was a product of 1879 state legislation that allowed "declarant" foreign-born persons the right to vote in state elections after residing in the state for one year. Such a provision was not unique to Louisiana; up until 1926, more than a dozen states nationwide offered "declarant permission" for voting (Keyssar 2000, table A.12, 337–39).[3] Yet, between 1885 and 1910, press discussions of the declarant aliens and immigrant franchise remained limited outside Louisiana (*Delta Independent* 1888; *Cañon City Record* 1908). Likewise, regional conversations appeared unconcerned with foreign-born voting so long as immigrants acquired US citizenship (Luconi 2004, 37). In Louisiana, however, not only did declarant aliens surface as a central issue in the contentious 1890s suffrage debates, Italian immigrants publicly and candidly joined the fray in proclaiming their opposition to disenfranchisement efforts.

Italian participation in Louisiana politics was neither new nor newly visible in New Orleans (*Daily Picayune* 1879; *Daily City Item* 1891; Nystrom 2010, 235). In the early 1870s, an Italian Club, 100 members strong, participated in a torchlight parade with other Reform Democrats (*Daily Picayune* 1872). In 1876, the Italian Legion, in white caps and blue capes and accompanied by musical bands and officer-laden carriages, joined thousands marching through central New Orleans; they processed with the "wildest enthusiasm" in opposition to the "frauds committed by the Radical Administration" (*Daily Picayune* 1876a, 1876b, 1876c). During the 1870s and 1880s, Italians organized throughout the city, from the Second, Third, Fifth, Sixth, and Tenth Wards, to promote naturalization and voter registration (*Daily Picayune* 1876b, 1876c, 1876d).

Following such precedents, on Sunday, March 22, 1896, a mass meeting of 2,000 Italians was held, conducted entirely in Italian, at Odd Fellows Hall on Camp Street in New Orleans (Burns 1963, 75). The site, known for hosting the Continental Guards clad in American Revolutionary soldier uniforms, offered a symbolic location for the Italian Club to elect their officers and for community leaders to deliver speeches. Among the speakers was Santo Oteri, an astoundingly wealthy and influential businessman who had realized community influence after taking over his Sicilian-born father's Central American fruit import business. Oteri encouraged participants to vote the Democratic Party line since, he explained, the Democrats had "always looked to [our] interest" (*Daily Picayune* 1896c; *Biographical and Historical Memoirs of Louisiana* 1892). Oteri went on to exploit the rhetoric and imagery of Italian nationalism: "As [we] remember the glorious deeds of Victor Emmanuel, Garibaldi and other distinguished patriots of [our] native land and revere them, [we] should fire [our] patriotism and stand united in a solid phalanx and vote for the regular Democratic ticket at the next election" (*Daily Picayune* 1896b). So too did Joseph di Carlo, the elected president of the proceedings, invoke the imagery of Italian nationalism when he described the impending "hot" campaign and encouraged participants to "see to it that the result was different from the Italian campaign in Africa" (*Daily Picayune* 1896b). With both Sicilians and other Italians present at the meeting, calling on figures of the Italian risorgimento and reminding audience members of the nationally embarrassing, failed invasion of Ethiopia (1895–1896), reflected the "Italianizing" of Sicilian immigrants and emerging *italianitá* within New Orleans's Italian immigrant community. The Italian Club proceeded to pass a series of resolutions, including one committing and pledging themselves to vote the Democratic Party line and support the Democratic candidate Murphy Foster for governor (*Daily Picayune* 1896d). After encouraging participants to commit to helping "the party which helps the Italians" (*Daily Picayune* 1896b; Scarpaci 1980, 281), the meeting adjourned, though their demonstrating continued as the gathering moved into the streets and culminated in a "festive" parade.

Subsequently dubbed the "Dago Parade" (see Figure 3) at least fifty Italians on heavy draft horses made their way through the streets of New Orleans; the "thundering of the hoofs on the pavements sounded like the march of two or three regiments of cavalry" (*Daily Picayune* 1896b). Marchers "promiscuously" shot off fireworks and carried lanterns, sticks, and banners, one of which even had a live rooster perched upon it. They carried additional roosters in birdcages and "perched on staffs," while at least a dozen goats accompanied the procession, "some of them being led along and others carried in a wagon, and allowed to feed on flowers" (*Daily Picayune* 1896b). Parading beneath an Italian flag, participants carried banners that read, in English, "Down with the suffrage amendment," "We are Democrats and not grasshoppers," and "We demand that the mechanic, the clerk and the laborer, white and black, have the same privilege to cast his ballot on election day as the millionaire" (*Daily Picayune* 1896b; Democratic Party [La.] State Central Committee 1898).

New Orleans newspapers did not report favorably on the Italian meeting and the Dago Parade. Estimating that "one-half of them did not know what they were there for," the *Picayune* characterized the participants at the meeting as too "enthusiastic" (*Daily Picayune* 1896b). Noting the use of "profane language," the press described the events as an uncivilized display of "rowdyism" and a "disgraceful spectacle." The amassed were "the sorriest looking set of citizens that anybody would care to rest their eye on" and "a disgrace to a civilized community" (*Daily Picayune* 1896b).

Despite certain protestations to the contrary, the paper employed ethnic stereotypes, explicitly noting the "foreignness" of the meeting. The Daily *Picayune* explained that the act of parading beneath the Italian flag offered evidence to support amending the state's suffrage and naturalization laws: "How long do you suppose they would remain here, if they manage to accumulate a few dollars? Why, they will go back to Italy, and there live in comparative luxury for the rest of their days" (*Daily Picayune* 1896b). Emphasizing the fact that "No English was Spoken," the story characterized the meeting as dangerous and uncivilized, since only a person with "some knowledge of the English language" could rise "above the level of a four-footed animal" (*Daily Picayune* 1896b; *Times Democrat* 1896a, 1896b). In contrast to rhetoric from the 1870s and 1880s, supporters of disenfranchisement in 1890s Louisiana invoked the long-standing (northern) stereotypes and perception of the Italian immigrant as a temporary sojourner, a "bird of passage," as fodder for suffrage constraints. Local politician Capt. William C. Dufour, capitalizing on existing xenophobic tropes, asserted that participants at the meeting were "ignorant, brutal and alien [and] did not even know or understand why they were called together for speech and for parade" (*Daily Picayune* 1896a). Just as anti-Italian discourse emerged locally in the postlynching era to justify the violence, the disenfranchisement debates similarly adopted anti-Italian language common in the national press to delegitimize the Italian meeting and substantiate voter restriction. Criticism leveled against the Dago Parade exploited questions of loyalty and citizenship and invoked existing xenophobic tropes in order to lend credence to a political critique of boss-ism and the Regular Democrats.

The ballot-reform debates were temporarily put on hold until the state constitutional convention in 1898, where the suffrage amendment proposed an educational qualification or literacy test; however, for those unable to meet the educational qualification, the proposal included a series of additional entitlements for the franchise, including eligibility based on property ownership. So expansive were the exemptions that the *Times Democrat* proclaimed that the "Monstrous Suffrage Plan" had created a series of "electoral freaks and monstrosities" (*Times Democrat* 1898b, 1898c). The negotiation of voting access for the state's "electoral freaks and monstrosities" reveals the racial and civic repercussions of expanding Italian voting rights within the disenfranchisement efforts of post–Reconstruction Louisiana.

Initially, the controversial Section 5 exemptions also included the following provision: "No male person of foreign birth, who shall have been naturalized prior to the adoption of this constitution, shall ever be denied the right to register and vote in this state by reason of his failure to possess the educational or property qualifications" (*Daily Picayune* 1898c). Louisiana's English-language press subsequently dubbed the provision the Privileged Dago clause, as the suffrage amendment—and foreign voting rights in general—became a source of statewide debate for weeks (*Times Democrat* 1898c, 1898d).

Calling it an "insult," an "injustice," a "scandal," the *Times Democrat* maintained that the provision was a "glaring show of partiality in favor of the illiterate and naturalized foreigner as against the illiterate of native birth" (*Times Democrat* 1898b, 1898e, 1898f). The *Monroe News* suggested that the suffrage amendment was "simply and solely a petty fogging trick intended to permit a lot of illiterates and riffraffs, whose skin happens to be white, to vote, whether they know what a ballot is or not" (*Monroe News* in *Daily Picayune* 1898d). By censuring the Privileged Dago clause for enfranchising "a lot of ignorant Dagoes and shut[ting] out a great many whites," opponents challenged the very place of Italians within a "white man's" government (*Lake Charles Press* in *Daily Picayune* 1898d). Dismissing the legal consideration of Italian whiteness, critics noted, "When we speak of a white man's government, [Italians] are as black as the blackest Negro in existence" (*Times Democrat* 1898g). Some Reformers even suggested that Black voters were preferable to Italian voters. Such opinions criticized the suffrage amendment, because it desired to make citizens of the "Dagoes . . . and disfranchise the Negro, and God knows if there is any difference between them it is largely in the darkies' favor" (*Franklin News* in *Times Democrat* 1898h). Grounded in an understanding of the Black vote as being more easily controlled, such palpably racist language designated the foreign vote as considerably more dangerous and disregarded the legal whiteness of Italians. This explicit denial of Italian whiteness wherein the racial questionability of Italians overshadowed their skin that "happen[ed] to be white," like the very act of lynching, collapsed Italians' race and color and constructed Dagoes in opposition to and outside whiteness (*Monroe News* in *Daily Picayune* 1898d).

Convention legislators eventually passed a suffrage amendment that included a residency requirement, a literacy provision, a property requirement (ownership of at least $300), and a poll tax. Despite the at times hostile anti-Italian remarks during the 1890s debates and a certain sentiment that cautioned against trusting "white" foreigners to vote, the Louisiana convention passed the Privileged Dago clause. The final iteration of the controversial and hotly debated clause specifically granted "male person[s] of foreign birth," if he were naturalized before January 1, 1898, the right to register and vote in the state of Louisiana even if he did not meet the literacy and property requirements (*Daily Picayune* 1898e; *Times Democrat* 1898i; Scarpaci 2003). Because "Sicilians nearly all voted the Democratic ticket and were good citizens," legislators, led by Ring Democrats (a faction of Louisiana's splintered Democratic party made up of professional politicians and ethnic ward bosses who practiced classic urban machine politics), protected foreign and Italian voting rights over the voting rights of Black southerners (*Daily Picayune* 1898a). The preservation of Italian voting functioned as a product of certain legislators recognizing Italians as useful constituents and voters. Regardless of opinions that problematized the racial position of Italians, Italians remained enfranchised, collapsing their race and color in the name of "home rule."

These disenfranchisement debates reveal that Italians in Louisiana were available pawns within local politicking. Those who contested the Privileged Dago clause (Reform Democrats) articulated their opposition in terms of rightful citizenship, loyalty, xenophobia, and racial questionability, all of which garnered publicly consumable support to eliminate the political machine. Others who favored the Privileged Dago clause (Regular Democrats) did so because of the professed political functionality of Italians; the efficacy of Italians compelled Regulars to protect the Italian voting bloc and their constituent base. Italians retained their right to vote in Louisiana not because of their racial acceptability or elevated status but because of their value in serving the (Regular) Democratic machine.

Ultimately, while not resulting in their systematized or institutionalized Jim Crow segregation, Louisiana social convention, legal practice, and print discourse variously denied Sicilians and other Italians access to informal citizenship and marked them as racially transient. Native-born, white Louisianans racially categorized Italians differently, sometimes as white and sometimes not, in different moments and for different reasons. Historically accounting for time and place—in moments of violence and political contestations—reinforces the contextual contingency of Italian racialization. Juxtaposing the Privileged Dago clause and the preservation of Italian voting rights in 1898 Louisiana with the 1899 Tallulah lynching of the five Sicilians "on behalf of white supremacy" further exposes the commutability of Italian racial construction.

Employing Natalia Molina's (2014) concept of "racial scripts," which speaks to the discursive continuity of racial projects across time and space, reveals how Louisianians both advanced and denied Italians the privileges of citizenship by employing (or countering) the same racial scripts used to marginalize Black southerners. Similarly, transnational anti-Sicilian and anti-Southern Italian dialogue and northern anti-Italian nativism also operated as racial scripts, which communities in Louisiana weaponized in various times and places to justify violence against and validate the subordinate status of Sicilians and other Italians. Focusing on scripts of citizenship incorporates the political and economic factors that underwrote contestations over Sicilian and Italian citizenship identities, while the context of Louisiana print culture highlights the duality that Sicilians and other Italians were both privileged as "white" Italians and marginalized—in violently real and racially discursive ways—as racially suspect Dagoes. In this way, because of their racial mobility and racial transiency and through their efforts in navigating the Louisiana racial structure, Italian immigrants—and the circulating language of race—in turn contributed to the codification of Jim Crow.

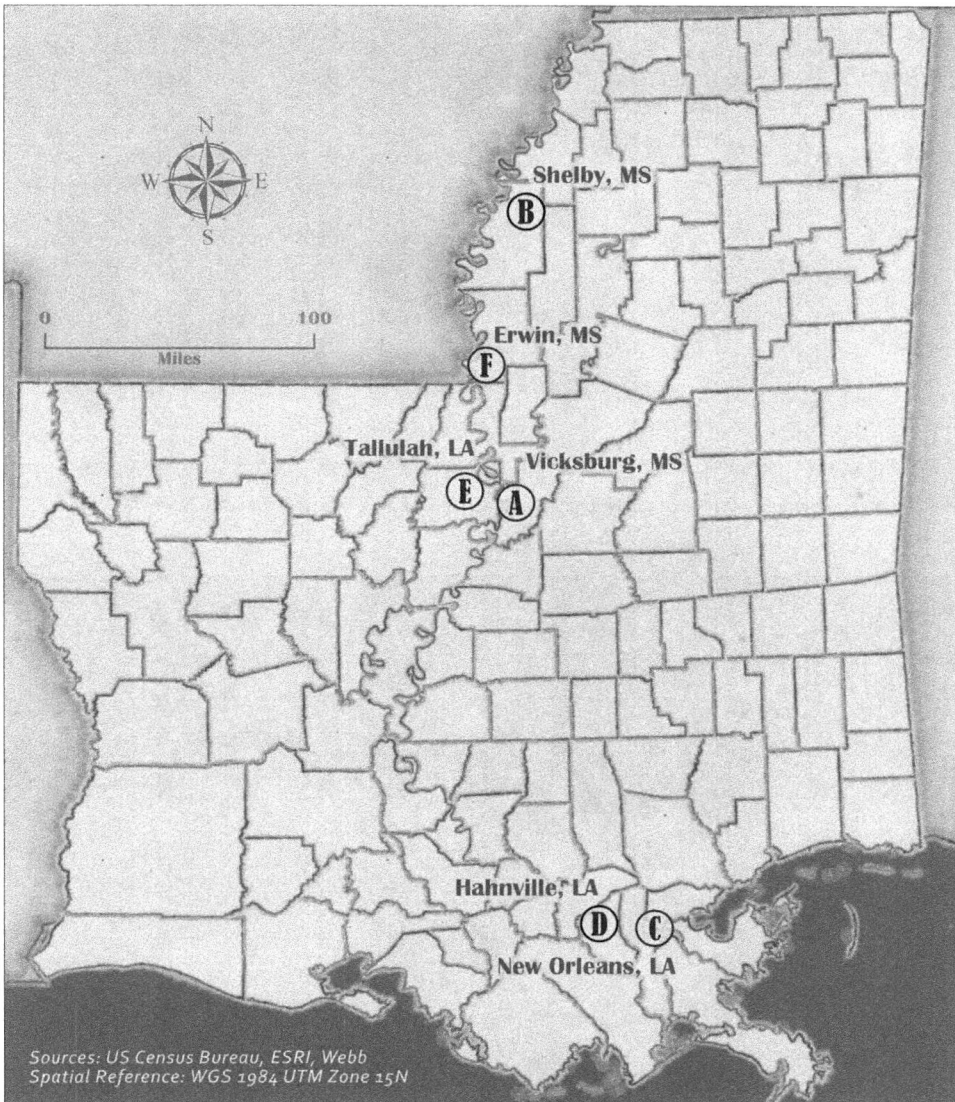

Map 3. Lynching of Italians/ Sicilians in LA and MS 1886 - 1901

Figure 1. Locations of lynchings of Sicilians and other Italians in Louisiana and Mississippi between 1886 and 1901. *A*, Vicksburg, MS (March 28, 1886): Federico Villarosa. *B*, Shelby, MS (June 11, 1887): "Dago Joe." *C*, New Orleans, LA (March 14, 1891): Antonio Bagnetto, James Caruso, Loreto Comitis, Rocco Geraci, Joseph P. Macheca, Antonio Marchesi, Pietro Monasterio, Emmanuele Polizzi, Frank Romero, Antonio Scaffidi, Charles Traina. *D*, Hahnville, LA (August 9, 1896): Salvatore Arena, Lorenzo Salardino, Giuseppe Venturella. *E*, Tallulah, LA (July 22, 1899): Giovanni Cerami, Carlo Difatta, Francesco Difatta, Giuseppe Difatta, Rosario Fiducia. *F*, Erwin, MS (July 11, 1901): Giovanni Serio, Vincenzo Serio.

FRANK DE FATTA.
With whom the Trouble began.

JOE DE FATTA.
Who shot Dr. Hodge.

ROSARIO FIDUCIA,
A Cousin of the De Fattas.

RECENT LYNCHING OF ITALIANS AT TALLULAH, LOUISIANA—THREE OF THE VICTIMS.—[SEE PAGE 779.]

Figure 2. Rare photographs of three of the lynching victims, Tallulah, LA (*Harper's Weekly* 1899, 765).

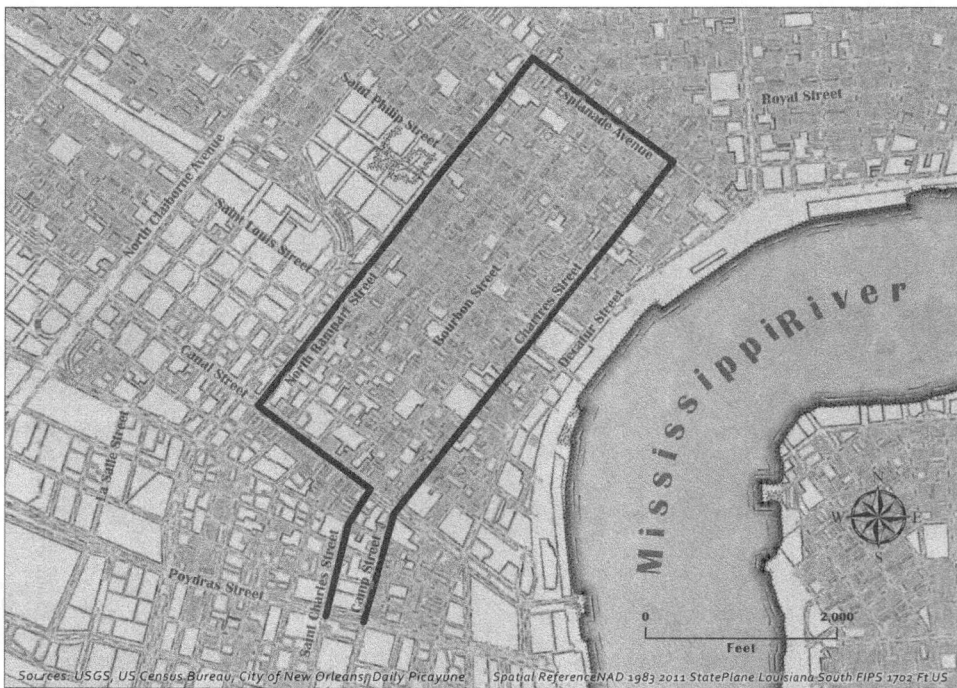

Map 4. Route of the 'Dago Parade' - a demonstration against Louisiana's proposed disenfranchisement efforts in 1896.

Figure 3. Route of the "Dago Parade" on March 21, 1896. Marching in opposition to Louisiana's proposed disenfranchisement efforts, Italians publicly demonstrated across New Orleans's French Quarter (*Daily Picayune* 1896b).

## Notes

[1] This essay is derived from portions of the author's previously published book *Dixie's Italians: Sicilians, Race, and Citizenship in the Jim Crow Gulf South* (Baton Rouge: Louisiana University Press, 2020). Thank you to LSU Press for granting permission to republish in this volume.

[2] The term *in-betweenness* originally appeared in John Higham's *Strangers in the Land* (1963, 169). See also Vellon (2010, 27). Throughout, I employ "inbetween" (in quotation marks and without the hyphen) in reference to this scholarship.

[3] During the nineteenth century, declarant aliens were allowed to vote in the following states: Alabama, Arkansas, Colorado, Florida, Georgia, Indiana, Kansas, Louisiana, Minnesota, Missouri, Montana, Nebraska, North Dakota, Oregon, South Dakota, and Texas; "declarant permission" was terminated in all of these states by 1926 (Keyssar 2000, table A.12, 337–339).

## Works Cited

*Arkansas Gazette*. 1899. "Hung Five." July 23, 1899.

Arnesen, Eric. 2001. "Whiteness and the Historians' Imagination." *International Labor and Working-Class History*. 60: 3–32.

Bailey, Amy Kate and Stewart Tolnay. 2015. *Lynched: The Victims of Southern Mob Violence.* Chapel Hill: University of North Carolina Press.

Barrett, James and David Roediger. 1997. "Inbetween Peoples: Race, Nationality and the 'New Immigrant' Working Class." *Journal of American Ethnic History.* 16, no. 3 (Spring): 101–140.

*Biloxi Daily Herald*. 1907. "Gov. Vardaman Denies the Story." December 31, 1907.

*Biographical and Historical Memoirs of Louisiana: Embracing an Authentic and Comprehensive Account of the Chief Events in the History of the State, a Special Sketch of Every Parish and a Record of the Lives of Many of the Most Worthy and Illustrious Families and Individuals*. 1892. vol 2. Chicago: Goodspeed Publishing.

Brodkin, Karen. 1998. *How Jews Became White Folks and What That Says about Race in America*. New Brunswick, NJ: Rutgers University Press.

Burns, Francis P. 1963. "St. Patrick's Hall and Its Predecessor, Odd Fellows Hall." *Louisiana History: The Journal of the Louisiana Historical Association*. 4, no. 1: 73–84.

*Cañon City Record*. 1908. "Criminal Offense to Vote Without Papers." May 21, 1908.*Columbus Dispatch*. 1907. "Remarkable Race Prejudice." October 17, 1907.

Cunningham, George. 1965. "The Italian, a Hindrance to White Solidarity in Louisiana, 1890–1898." *Journal of Negro History*. 50, no. 1 (January): 22–36.

*Daily City Item*. 1891. October 28, 1891.

*Daily Picayune*. 1872. The Grand Procession." August 11, 1872.

*Daily Picayune*. 1876a. "City Politics." August 27, 1876.

*Daily Picayune*. 1876b. "City Politics." August 31, 1876.

*Daily Picayune*. 1876c. "The Italian Legion." September 21, 1876.

*Daily Picayune*. 1876d. "Political." August 26, 1876.

*Daily Picayune*. 1879. "In the City." September 30, 1879.

*Daily Picayune*. 1889. "Our Italian Fellow-Citizens." March 4, 1889.

*Daily Picayune*. 1895. "Italian Immigration." January 15, 1895.

*Daily Picayune*. 1896a. "Citizens Not to Be Trusted." March 25, 1896.

*Daily Picayune*. 1896b. "The March of the Regulars." April 19, 1896.

*Daily Picayune*. 1896c. "Italian Regulars paraded by the Ring, After a Meeting at Which No English Was Spoken." March 23, 1896.

*Daily Picayune*. 1896d. "Mauberret's Italians: Opposed to Suffrage Amendments and Independent Movements." February 25, 1896.

*Daily Picayune*. 1898a. "Suffrage Plan to Be Repaired." March 12, 1898.

*Daily Picayune*. 1898b. March 16, 1898.

*Daily Picayune*. 1898c. "Text of the Suffrage Plan Prepared by the Sub-Committee of Six; The Weeks Plans of Enfranchising All Who Were Voters." March 2, 1898.

*Daily Picayune*. 1898d. "Louisiana Opinions, What the Newspapers of This Great State Have Said." March 15, 1898.

*Daily Picayune*. 1898e. "Agreement Reached." March 25, 1898.

*Daily Picayune*. 1899. "Lynching of Sicilians at Tallulah." July 22, 1899.

*Daily States*. 1899a. July 24, 1899.

*Daily States*. 1899b. July 27, 1899.

*Daily States*. 1899c. July 22, 1899.

*Delta Independent*. 1888. "How Foreign-Born Persons May Acquire Title to Public Land." September 4, 1888.

Democratic Party (La.) State Central Committee. 1898. *The Convention of '98: A Complete Work on the Greatest Political Event in Louisiana's History, and a Sketch of the Men Who Composed It. Together with a Historical Review of the Conventions of the Past, and the General Assembly Which Called the Constitutional Convention of 1898*. New Orleans: W. E. Myers, 1898.

Fields, Barbara. 2001. "Whiteness, Racism, and Identity." *International Labor and Working-Class History*. 60: 48–56.

Guglielmo, Thomas. 2003. *White on Arrival: Italians, Race, Color, and Power in Chicago, 1890–1945*. New York: Oxford University Press.

Guterl, Matthew. 2001. *The Color of Race in America, 1900–1940*. Cambridge, MA: Harvard University Press.

Hale, Grace Elizabeth. 1999. *Making Whiteness: The Culture of Segregation in the South, 1890–1940*. New York: Vintage Books.

*Harper's Weekly*. 1899. "Recent Lynching of Italians at Tallulah, Louisiana—Three of the Victims." August 5, 1899. 43, no. 2224, 759–780.

Harris, Cheryl I. 1993. "Whiteness as Property." *Harvard Law Review*. 106, no. 8 (June): 1707–1791.

Higham, John. 1963. *Strangers in the Land*. New York: Atheneum.

Jackson, Jessica Barbata. 2017. "Before the Lynching: Reconsidering the Experience of Italians and Sicilians in Louisiana, 1870s–1890s." *Louisiana History: The Journal of the Louisiana Historical Association*. 58, no. 3 (Summer): 300–338.

Jackson, Jessica Barbata. 2020. *Dixie's Italians: Sicilians, Race, and Citizenship in the Jim Crow Gulf South*. Baton Rouge: Louisiana State University Press.

Jacobson, Matthew Frye. 1998. *Whiteness of a Different Color: European Immigrants and the Alchemy of Race*. Cambridge, MA: Harvard University Press.

Keyssar, Alexander. 2000. *The Right to Vote: The Contested History of Democracy in the United States*. New York: Basic Books.

Lopez, Ian Haney. 1996. *White by Law: The Legal Construction of Race*. New York: New York University Press.

Luconi, Stefano. 2004. *The Italian-American Vote in Providence, Rhode Island, 1916–1948*. Cranbury, NJ.: Rosemont Publishing.

Luconi, Stefano. 2013. "The Lynching of Italian Americans: A Reassessment." In *Selected Essays from the 42nd Annual Conference of the American Italian Historical Association, Held October 29–31, 2009, in Baton Rouge, Louisiana*, edited by Alan J Gravano, Ilaria Serra, and American Italian Historical Association. New York: John D. Calandra Italian-American Institute.

*Notes from the Italian Legation in the U.S. to the Department of State, #1739*. "G. C. Vinci Letter to U.S. Secretary of State John Hay." July 25, 1899a.

*Notes from the Italian Legation in the U.S. to the Department of State, #1739.* "Report by the Secretary of the Royal Embassy at Washington Camillo Romano." August 1, 1899b.

*Notes from the Italian Legation in the U.S. to the Department of State, #1739.* "Fava to U.S. Secretary of State John Hay." January 15, 1900.

Nystrom, Justin. 2010. *New Orleans after the Civil War: Race, Politics, and a New Birth of Freedom.* Baltimore: Johns Hopkins University Press.

*Papers Relating to the Foreign Relations of the United States, Transmitted to Congress, With the Annual Message of the President.* 1899. Washington, DC: Government Printing Office.

Roediger, David. 2005. *Working toward Whiteness: How America's Immigrants Became White, The Strange Journey from Ellis Island to the Suburbs.* New York: Basic Books.

Roediger, David. 2007. *The Wages of Whiteness: Race and the Making of the American Working Class,* rev. ed. London: Verso.

Scarpaci, Vincenza. 1980. *Italian Immigrants in Louisiana's Sugar Parishes: Recruitment, Labor Conditions, and Community Relations, 1880–1910.* New York: Arno Press.

Scarpaci, Vincenza. 2003. "Walking the Color Line: Italian Immigrants in Rural Louisiana, 1880–1910." In *Are Italians White? How Race Is Made in America,* edited by Jennifer Guglielmo and Salvatore Salerno, 60–76. New York: Routledge.

*Times Democrat.* 1896a. "Sunday's Italian Parade." March 24, 1896.

*Times Democrat.* 1896b. "The Late Italian Parade." April 4, 1896.

*Times Democrat.* 1898a. "Suffrage Plan to Be Repaired." March 12, 1898.

*Times Democrat.* 1898b. "Monstrous Suffrage Plan." March 3, 1898.

*Times Democrat.* 1898c. "Editorial." March 7, 1898.

*Times Democrat.* 1898d. "Insult to Native Citizens." March 8, 1898.

*Times Democrat.* 1898e. "Insult to Native-Born Citizens." March 5, 1898.

*Times Democrat.* 1898f. "Insult to Native Citizens." March 6, 1898.

*Times Democrat.* 1898g. "Louisiana Affairs." March 22, 1898.

*Times Democrat.* 1898h. March 22, 1898.

*Times Democrat.* 1898i. "Agreement Reached." March 25, 1898.

*Times Democrat.* 1898j. "Popular Protests." March 8, 1898.

*Times Democrat.* 1898k. "More Protests." March 9, 1898.

*Times Democrat.* 1898l. "The Suffrage." March 13, 1898.

*Times Democrat.* 1899a. July 21, 1899.

*Times Democrat.* 1899b. "Tallulah Lynching. Italians Had Planned a Plot to Murder. Conspiracy Clearly Shown by the Trend of Events. The Dead Men All Had Blackened Records. One of the Remaining Italians Left the Parish Hurriedly." July 23, 1899.

*Times Democrat.* 1899c. "Citizens Plead Necessity for White Supremacy." July 25, 1899.

*Times Democrat.* 1899d. "Five Italians Lynched." July 22, 1899.

*Times Democrat.* 1899e. "Tallulah Tragedy." July 28, 1899.

Vellon, Peter G. 2010. "'Between White Men and Negroes': The Perception of Southern Italian Immigrants through the Lens of Italian Lynchings." In *Anti-Italianism: Essays on a Prejudice,* edited by William J. Connell and Fred Gardaphé. Basingstoke, UK: Palgrave Macmillan.

Webb, Clive. 2008. "The Lynching of Sicilian Immigrants in the American South, 1886–1910." In *Lynching Reconsidered: New Perspectives in the Study of Mob Violence,* edited by William D. Carrigan, 175–204. New York: Routledge.

*Weekly Messenger.* 1891. March 21, 1891.

# The Original Dixieland Jazz Band, the Black/Italian Racial Nexus, and Transatlantic Jazz Historiography

JOHN GENNARI

## I

In February of 1917, the Original Dixieland Jass (later Jazz) Band, a quintet of white New Orleans musicians led by James Dominick (Nick) LaRocca, the son of Sicilian immigrants, made what most jazz historians have regarded as the first jazz phonograph record, a 78-rpm shellac disc produced by the Victor Talking Machine Co., with "Dixie Jazz Band One-Step" on the A side and "Livery Stable Blues" on the B side. The ODJB had arrived in New York City just weeks earlier for an engagement at Reisenweber's Cafe on Columbus Circle, playing up-tempo foxtrots and one-steps, slow blues grinds, and other dances white college kids and twentysomethings quickly embraced, keen for an alternative to the waltzing violins favored by their parents. This was only a year after an earlier iteration of the ensemble had come north to Chicago for an extended gig at a dive called Schiller Cafe before moving over to the classier gangster-operated Casino Gardens, whose clientele included such vaudeville stars as Bert Williams, Fanny Brice, Will Rogers, Buster Keaton, and a young upstart named Al Jolson. Jolson, turned on by the music, prevailed upon his New York manager to push the band, resulting in the coveted Reisenweber booking. So immediate and intense was the Dixieland buzz on Broadway that Columbia Records signed the ODJB to a contract only a week into the engagement and quickly cut two records. Columbia disliked the result; they shelved the project and left the field open to their major competitor, Victor, whose executives, having made good money on their Enrico Caruso and John Philip Sousa discs, were also leery of the strange sounds captured by their recording engineer (Bomberger 2018, 44–47; Carney 2009, 47–49; Charters 2008, 126–157; Wald 2009, 49–50).

As it happened, "Livery Stable Blues" vaulted to fame overnight, owing in large part to its simulated animal sounds: a rooster crow by clarinetist Larry Shields, a horse whinny by LaRocca, and a donkey bray by slide trombonist Eddie "Daddy" Edwards. Such novelty effects were typical of old-fashioned minstrel show hokum, a tradition not unfamiliar to the ODJB. Despite its title, the tune bore little resemblance to the blues, in part because Victor pushed the band to play it— this was true of "Dixie Band One-Step" as well—faster than they were accustomed lest the music not fit onto the shellac disc. What came through to listeners was the band's raucous energy, peppy spirit, driving rhythm, and unbridled enthusiasm. This felt modern and liberating, especially to the millions of young people on both sides of the Atlantic whose lives were being upended by the Great War.

The ODJB was a multiethnic proletarian outfit: Like LaRocca, Tony Sbabaro, the band's drummer, was Sicilian; Shields and Edwards, the clarinetist and trombonist, were Irish. Each came from a working-class family. LaRocca's father was a shoemaker, Nick himself trained in the construction trades, and in just a few years he would quit the music business and return to New Orleans to build houses. But in 1917, in one of the watershed moments of modern culture, the band triggered a pop culture craze that prefigured the Jazz Age of the 1920s, with its flappers, gangsters, speakeasies, Charlie Chaplin, Greta Garbo, and Rudolph Valentino.

## II

I cannot think of another musical genre so out of keeping with contemporary progressive sensibilities as Dixieland jazz. The very name conjures an iconography of the Old South that most everyone except the alt-right and the fashion conscious would be happy to see disappear: Confederate flags, parasol parades, striped suits, boater hats. And yet the music continues to be performed by excellent musicians and brings considerable pleasure to audiences in the US and abroad, many of them both racial liberals and dues-paying members of their local Dixieland Jazz Society. Even before the racial reckoning triggered by George Floyd's murder, these societies had been engaged in a robust debate about whether the stigma attached to the word *Dixieland* had become so harmful as to warrant its once-and-for-all replacement by other of the music's monikers, such as *traditional jazz, trad,* or *hot jazz.* This is an issue one might expect to have been settled a long time ago, when some of the very few African American musicians still working in the idiom (such as those associated with Preservation Hall) began to insist that what they performed was New Orleans jazz, not *Dixieland,* a word they saw as catering to the nostalgic desires of white listeners keen on remembering the 1920s for its devil-may-care frolic and not for the resurgence of the Ku Klux Klan. The fact that Louis Armstrong, the great master of traditional New Orleans jazz, often used the word *Dixieland* and made recordings with groups like the Dukes of Dixieland, was one of the main reasons he fell out of favor with many younger, civil rights-minded African Americans of the WWII and postwar generations.

This paper is an effort to sort through the original ODJB's fraught and ambivalent place in jazz history and what it tells us about jazz, race, and the cultural politics of the Black/Italian nexus. I will examine these issues in a transatlantic and transhistorical framework, moving first from jazz's blossoming in early-twentieth-century New Orleans, to its commercialization in New York City on the eve of the Jazz Age, to its perhaps surprising emergence in pre–World War II Fascist Italy. Within this temporal frame, I will narrate how the ODJB quickly attained international celebrity status, disbanded, and briefly but unsuccessfully reassembled at a time when Italy's invasion of Ethiopia had complicated relations between African Americans and Italian Americans. I will examine how jazz's reception and development in Italy fit into broader cultural and ideological currents in Europe and how the nascent fields of jazz criticism and historiography, in assessing the ODJB's role in early jazz, engaged in a consequential effort to frame issues of race as central to an understanding of jazz. Then I will consider the cultural memory of the ODJB with a special focus on the vexed US ethnic politics shaping efforts to commemorate Nick LaRocca and a striking irony in the way LaRocca has been memorialized in Italy. Finally, I will offer some concluding thoughts about the significance of American popular music and race in this moment of resurgent white nationalism and fascism. There are a lot of moving parts to my analysis and a density of historical detail I hope is not overwhelming. My intention is not just to advance our understanding of the original ODJB and its legacy but to show how the fields of jazz studies and Italian American and Italian diasporic studies can be put into productive dialogue.

I refer to the *original* ODJB because the band has been playing for more than a century with changing personnel, most recently under the leadership of Jimmy LaRocca, Nick's son, a fine musician in his own right. Despite the band's longevity and its many successes, however, the original unit's reputation as jazz antiheroes—or as a distraction from more important musicians and "real" jazz history—continues to endure (Leo 2018, 39–44). Many have derided the ODJB as a reactionary minstrelsy outfit that capitalized on the racial bias of the nascent recording industry to eclipse the groundbreaking jazz played by superior Black musicians—a position LaRocca did little to discourage when, from the 1930s until his death in 1961, he petulantly disparaged Black musicians and insisted that jazz was an entirely white invention. LaRocca argued that "the negro did not play any kind of music equal to white men at any time. Even the poorest band of white men played better than the negroes in my day." This appears in the transcript of one of the interviews LaRocca provided the Hogan Jazz Archive at Tulane University. At the end of that transcript, he describes African Americans as uncultured and "lazy," adding "I'm a segregationist and a die-hard one because I don't think the colored man has earned his place, so far. Maybe in the years to come, but not now" (LaRocca, WRHA interviews). This was 1959.

As I will later discuss in more detail, the marginalization of the ODJB started in the mid-1920s, when jazz's most popular form in both the US and abroad was a symphonic style associated with bandleader Paul Whiteman, whose name and persona signified a decisive shift in the music away from its southern, interracial, working-class, and folkloric roots. This whitening of jazz happened at the very time Joe "King" Oliver, Freddie Keppard, Jelly Roll Morton, Sidney Bechet, Louis Armstrong, and other Black musicians from New Orleans were cutting records that only later displaced the ODJB, Whiteman, and other white musicians in the jazz canon. The now virtually undisputed idea that African American musicians were jazz's originators and key innovators would not become ascendant until the 1930s. That was when a handful of pioneering European and American critics began to define jazz authenticity with two main criteria: anti-commercialism, and rootedness in Black culture. Like Whiteman, LaRocca was nothing if not commercially oriented. Unlike Whiteman, LaRocca did not adjust to jazz's new ideological environment in the 1930s; in fact, on the key question of jazz's racial provenance, he positioned himself as one of its staunchest outliers and resisters.

Needless to say, LaRocca is a glaring exception to the tradition of Black/Italian cultural affinity, stylistic rapport, and personal intimacy exemplified in the well-known relationships between Louis Prima and Louis Armstrong; iconic Italian American singers such as Frank Sinatra and Tony Bennett and a number of major Black jazz musicians (Armstrong, Billie Holiday, Lester Young, Count Basie, Miles Davis, Quincy Jones); Dion DiMucci and other Italian doo-wop performers and their Black counterparts and collaborators; the Rascals' Felix Cavaliere and Motown's Smoky Robinson; Bruce Springsteen and Clarence Clemons—the list goes on (Gennari 2017, 29–71). Underlying such connections is a long history of musical exchange between North Africa and Southern Italy. The pioneering American ethnomusicologist Alan Lomax discovered as much in his field work in Campania, where he found a group of Italian musicians he described as a "genuine North-African orchestra composed of drums, scrapers, rattles, clappers and tambourine" playing a tarantella (Celenza 2017, 12). In New Orleans, Sicilian open-air festa bands, funeral corteges, and Catholic saint's day celebrations joined US military bands, wagon advertisements, and African American second-line parades to make the city's streets the most polyphonic and polyrhythmic in the Western Hemisphere. Bruce Boyd Raeburn, former curator of the Hogan Archive, coined the phrase "bel canto meets the funk" to characterize a Black/Italian New Orleans synthesis of melodic beauty and earthy, sensual vitality, a joining of lyricism and rhythmic groove that has been an essential feature of jazz, R&B, doo-wop, and soul (Raeburn 2014).

LaRocca's anti-Black bigotry, denial of Black musical influence (despite ample evidence to the contrary), and segregationist sentiment were not atypical of white musicians who authored the style that became known as Dixieland. When jazz historian Burton Peretti defines Dixieland as a "syncopated style of white band music that grew up alongside New Orleans black jazz," he is pointing to the fact that the musical culture of New Orleans was not exempt from the city's broader racialized economic and political structures (Peretti 1994, 76). Entertainment was in fact a central pillar of the local economy. Music was a labor market, and like other of the city's labor markets, it was deeply segregated. Peretti points to the example of white bandleader George "Papa" Laine, an employer and mentor to LaRocca and many other Italian American musicians, who hired a man for one of his bands, "but when I found out he was a n-----, that's when I stopped hiring him. … I never knew he was colored. … [But] one fine day I passed on Ursuline Street, where he lived, and I saw his daddy and that was enough." For reasons both economic and cultural, Creoles of color were no less inclined to distance themselves from darker-skinned brethren. Jelly Roll Morton (né Ferdinand Joseph LaMothe) told Alan Lomax that his French Creole grandmother disowned him when she learned that he played "common music with the sons of fieldhands" (31).

Early New Orleans jazz developed in a local culture marked by intricate ethnoracial and class dynamics. On the one hand, New Orleans figures in jazz discourse as a uniquely pluralistic, polyglot environment: the nation's "oldest, most complex melting pot," a musical "gumbo." Such food metaphors often come with a positive, even romantic view of cross-cultural exchange, such as when Garry Boulard describes jazz as a means "to share vital experiences, appreciate each other's struggles, learn from one another artistically and musically, and join in a quiet alliance of social and political sympathy" (Boulard 1988, 64). Bruce Boyd Raeburn's painstaking research has painted a clear picture of the substantial Jewish and Sicilian presence in New Orleans's incipient jazz community. Musicians from these groups, he argues, along with Latinx and Afro-French Creole ones, "were able to create 'American' identities for themselves by assimilation to black vernacular musical practices through jazz" (Raeburn 2009, 124). Because of the broad popular appeal of New Orleans's many styles of music, from opera to parade music, most New Orleans musicians shrewdly recognized that learning to play as many idioms as possible was the best way to make a good living. If only for this practical reason, ethnic animosities, such as those between Creoles of color and African Americans, or those within the Sicilian community, sometimes were ameliorated on bandstands and dance floors and in street parades (Raeburn 2009, 134, 140).[1]

But New Orleans at the time of jazz's emergence was a deeply racist city where the Jim Crow color line was first legally codified and then brutally enforced for decades to come. Indeed, the incident that led to the 1896 *Plessy v. Ferguson* decision in which the US Supreme Court upheld the constitutionality of racial segregation was intimately connected to the New Orleans jazz community in its period of early formation. Daniel Desdunes was a well-known local musician who played in the Onward Brass Band, an important training ground for King Oliver and other budding jazz players. Desdunes was also a civil rights activist who had descended from a family of Creoles of color who had attained freedom before the Civil War. He volunteered to board a train car designated for whites in violation of Louisiana's 1890 Separate Car Act. This was to have been the test case enabling the Comité des Citoyens, a Creoles of color citizen's committee that included family members of Sidney Bechet, Armand Piron, Achille Baquet, and other renowned Creole jazz musicians, to challenge the law in courts. As it happened, the train Desdunes boarded was an interstate one, allowing a Louisiana court to dodge the case by ruling that the train was bound by federal law. Only then did the citizens committee turn to another mixed-race man, Homer Plessy. Plessy was arrested for boarding a "white" intrastate train and convicted in Judge John Howard Ferguson's court. The ruling was appealed but subsequently upheld in the state and federal Supreme Courts (Hersch 2007, 25).

One of the key consequences of *Plessy v. Ferguson* was the establishment of Local 174 of the American Federation of Musicians (AFM), whose charter restricted membership to "white musicians of southeastern Louisiana." It was not until 1926 that local African Americans had a permanent musicians union of their own, AFM Local 496 (Peretti 1994, 157). In the interim, first- and second-generation Italians and other white musicians profited from an acute disparity in employment opportunities, enabling them to perform in upscale hotels, concert halls, and other elite spaces closed off to Black people. What blues historian Tony Russell said about the shared musical heritage of Blacks and whites applied even more firmly to Jim Crow New Orleans: "[T]he barriers were not to fall; what God, in the eyes of the southern white man, had put asunder, no musical communion could join together" (33).

## III

Before LaRocca and company arrived in New York City, there were a handful of outfits in the United States calling themselves jazz (or jass or jasz) bands; within weeks there were dozens. Jazz-fad song titles soon flooded the market: "Jazzing Around," "At the Jazz Band Ball," "Some Jazz Blues," "New Orleans Jazz," "Everybody's Jazzing It," and "Oriental Jazz." Irving Berlin later expressed a distaste for jazz, but he struck while the iron was hot with a record titled "Mr. Jazz Himself." Thomas Edison joked that jazz records sounded better if you played them backward, but within a month of the ODJB Victor recordings, he brought singer Arthur Fields into his studio to wax a tune called "Everybody Loves a 'Jass' Band" (Wald 2009, 58).

The ODJB's engagement at Reisenweber's continued through most of 1917. Columbia's chastened management released the ODJB records they had recorded before the Victor ones struck gold, while the band also cut sides for the Aeolian-Vocalion label. All this activity received massive publicity, inspiring bands across the country to try to capitalize on the ODJB formula. Back in the Crescent City, cornetist Joe Oliver fired one of his sidemen so that his band would conform to the ODJB's five-piece configuration. The next several years found LaRocca and his bandmates in England, where they toured as "The Creators of Jazz." Their triumphs included a command performance for the royal family and the honor of playing at the gala Victory Ball following the signing of the Treaty of Versailles. The band recorded more records for English Columbia, including "Barnyard Blues," "Satanic Blues," and "Sensation Rag." These discs sold widely across the British Isles and the Continent, sparking a craze for dance music that led to bookings for other American bands and a wave of home-grown imitators (Bomberger 2018, 182–185; Carney 2009, 50–52; Brunn 1960, 124–140). In the inaugural issue of a London-based journal called *Palais Dancing News*, LaRocca was reported to have claimed that "jazz is the assassination, the murdering, the slaying of syncopation. … I even go so far as to confess we are musical anarchists" (Brunn 1960, 135).

LaRocca was as savvy a publicist as the fledgling jazz world had yet seen, but this was not enough to forestall a demise of the ODJB that had started in the heat of its blaze of glory. Daddy Edwards, the trombonist, was drafted into the Army in 1918; pianist Henry Ragas died of the Spanish flu in 1919; clarinetist Larry Shields quit in 1921, weary of the road. LaRocca replaced these musicians and kept the band going for another few years. But after suffering a nervous breakdown in 1925, he returned to New Orleans and took up full-time work in construction, as if he'd never been a musician.

By this time, Paul Whiteman had fully emerged as a bandleader, composer, violinist, and showman par excellence, becoming a household name in both the US and Europe. For many jazz musicians and historians, Whiteman personifies the wrongheadedness of the 1920s. These were the years when Louis Armstrong and Duke Ellington made the first of their classic records. And yet it was Whiteman, using his brilliant instincts for publicity, who crowned himself the "King of Jazz" and became the subject of a Hollywood movie of that name. Whiteman shrewdly leveraged the deeply ingrained cultural racism of the era by acknowledging Africa and Black culture as the seedbed of jazz while positioning himself as the primary agent of the music's legitimization as an important and respectable American music. In doing so, Whiteman established a template for the white appropriation of Black creativity that subsequently (and more familiarly) launched the careers of Benny Goodman and Elvis Presley. What this meant for African American musicians is an important and deceptively complex question; my focus here, however, is how Whiteman's ascendancy hinged on his aesthetic, ethno-racial, and class othering of the ODJB.

This happened first and most transparently in Whiteman's 1924 concert at New York's Aeolian Hall, famous for culminating in the debut of George Gershwin's "Rhapsody in Blue." Billed as an "Experiment in Modern Music," the concert was the first of several Whiteman would organize over the next fifteen years in which he narrated a history of jazz between numbers performed by his orchestra. The idea was to show that jazz had evolved from primitive beginnings as a crude, unwritten music performed by uneducated players in lowbrow dance halls and cabarets into one that was fully composed and performed by trained musicians in highbrow concert halls. Whiteman's formula is commonly construed as a derogation of Black musicians as purely instinctive, nonthinking bearers of a musical language that would require the intercession of putatively more sophisticated white musicians to reach its full potential. But the tune Whiteman chose to open the concert program and represent jazz's crass beginnings was "Livery Stable Blues," which the audience firmly associated with the ODJB (Wald 2009, 77–83; Dunkel 2021, 53–89).

Here is how one critic later described the Whiteman orchestra's rendition of "Livery Stable Blues": "Loud and boisterous playing with each horn baying after its own rabbit, freakish muted sounds, bewildering harmonies, thunderous barrelhouse piano, and explosive double drumming with clanging cowbells, clattering woodblocks, and crashing cymbals. It was energetic horseplay and the audience loved it" (quoted by Dunkel 2021, 66).

Whiteman, as was his wont, made a spectacle—a very particular kind of spectacle: a burlesque or a parody, not unlike minstrel shows in which white performers wearing blackface mocked actual Black people as loud, comical, carnal, and unsophisticated. Such performances—the bedrock of American entertainment going back to the 1830s—had the effect of confirming and reinforcing social, racial, and gender hierarchies.

The latter hinged on Whiteman's self-proclaimed mission to "make a lady out of jazz"—to rescue "Lady Jazz," that is, from the hypermasculine sporting-life environs in which the music had incubated in unsavory districts of New Orleans, San Francisco, and Chicago. Whiteman's feminization of jazz hinged on his own gender performance, which was multidimensional and hence now somewhat tricky to read retrospectively. Visually, on stage, and in public, Whiteman was a corpulent, tuxedoed, fastidiously coiffed dandy. But the sound of his voice betrayed his Denver upbringing and American Everyman persona. One of the most photographed men of his time, Whiteman projected images of both cosmopolitan sophistication and down-home midwestern American wholesomeness. His was a foursquare white American masculinity comfortably positioned in the national mythos in a way the second-generation Sicilian New Orleanian Nick LaRocca and his publicists could only envy.

Central to Whiteman's gender coding, jazz scholar Mario Dunkel argues, was the notion of the arranger/composer as a masculine artist who applies reason and intellect to the sonic chaos associated with an unruly feminized body. "Whiteman['s] jazz historiography," he writes, "reaffirmed the prevalent gendering of reason as a male-dominated quality, while feminizing the chaotic object to which it [was] applied" (69).[2] In other words, on the Aeolian Hall stage, Whiteman, in extricating "Lady Jazz" from the vulgar cacophony of the ODJB, elevated the music to its proper place—not just the concert hall setting, but also the sphere of textuality, the space where orality (the sounds produced by flesh-and-blood bodies) gets converted into *music* in the form of written scores and arrangements. This is what Whiteman meant when he claimed to be "put[ting] the music into jazz."

As became clear in the autobiography he co-authored with journalist Mary Margaret McBride—the book, published in 1926, was hubristically titled *Jazz*— Whiteman thought of himself as assuaging his middle-class audience's anxieties about the primitivism and hedonism associated with the forms of early jazz produced by lower-class Blacks and whites and patronized by the New Woman of the period who demanded sexual and social liberties. But it is not clear from the historical record that the Aeolian Hall audience was as keen as Whiteman to lift jazz into respectability or felt it needed to be protected from moral or aesthetic threats posed by the music. When critics noted that the audience loved the Whiteman orchestra's rendition of "Livery Stable Blues," they did not make clear whether this audience responded gleefully to the performance because they understood it to be a condescending parody, or because they were turned on by the tune in the same way audiences around the world had been when they first heard the ODJB's 1917 Victor recording.

## IV

At issue here was jazz's role as a conduit of urban modernity and as an aesthetic force within the larger modernist movement. The issue becomes more interesting when we examine it in a transatlantic frame. Anna Harwell Celenza, in her 2017 book *Jazz Italian Style: From Its Origins in New Orleans to Fascist Italy and Sinatra*, observes that whereas in France and Germany in the late 1910s and early 1920s jazz was seen as an "exotic, avant-garde art form performed almost exclusively by African Americans and rooted in a primitivist aesthetic," in Italy "listeners perceived jazz as a fully commercialized art form linked to wealth, modern technology, and Italian American innovation." Celenza shows that certain influential Italian artists and intellectuals, starting with the Futurists, embraced jazz as a "native" art form—an art that was Italian in spirit and marked from its emergence by Italian innovation—thereby setting the stage for Benito Mussolini's appropriation of the music as part of his Fascist cultural program. Jazz, Futurism, and Italian Fascism converged in a nexus of discourses emphasizing speed, vigor, courage, youth, energy, urbanism, machinery, and noise. Italy, the Futurist poet Filippo Tommaso Marinetti said, should be recognized as a modern nation and "not merely as a land of ruins and museums." Jazz, a new music for a modernizing nation, fit the bill perfectly (Celenza 2017, 23–24).

One of the defining characteristics of the interwar European avant-garde was a fascination with the seemingly oppositional realms of primitivism and machine-age modernity. This preoccupation was not exclusive to jazz, but it is striking how perfectly jazz fit the model of what Jeremy Lane calls the "techno-primitive hybrid" (Lane 2013, 3). In an aesthetic response to the shocks of war, imperialism, and industrial mechanization, modernist artists across media nurtured a potent fantasy of a primordial Africa married to a futuristic America. French poet Jean Cocteau, in a series of essays in 1918 and 1919, proposed a network of associations between what he saw as jazz's primeval rhythms and the formal purity of skyscrapers, ocean liners, and other icons of the American machine age. For the Swiss-French architect Le Corbusier, the sounds of jazz—which he loved—

expressed primitive Africa as well as "the grinding of tramways, the unbridled madness of the subway, the hammering of machines in factories" (Lane, 4).

Some European intellectuals used similar associations to express their horror at the emerging techno-cultural landscape. After touring the US to observe its industrial and technological developments and Jazz Age social mores, French doctor and novelist Georges Duhamel published a book called *America the Menace: Scenes from the Life of the Future* (1931) that became a best-seller in France. Duhamel was horrified by the mechanized slaughter he witnessed in the Chicago stockyards; he saw it as the epitome of modern industrial efficiency and likened it to the mass slaughter of uniformed infantrymen on the western front, where he had served as a medic during World War I. These scenes of primitive barbarity conjoined in Duhamel's fevered imagination with the sounds of jazz: The mechanized factory, the battlefield, the elevated railway, and the jazz nightclub fused into an overdetermined image of American machine-age dehumanization (Lane 2013, 1–3).

Italian Futurists like Marinetti and the painter and sculptor Umberto Boccioni were closer in their perceptions of jazz to Cocteau and other French primitivists who embraced the music's rhythmic and sonic properties and its association with American modern urbanism as a source of rejuvenation for tired, complacent, and backward-looking bourgeois society. Enthusiasm for jazz spread very quickly beyond artistic avant-garde circles to Italy's affluent elites. The music became the center of a burgeoning nightclub scene in Rome and all the major northern cities. New dance schools "sprouted like weeds across the urban landscape, promising step-by-step upward mobility for eager, aspiring socialites" (Celenza 2017, 48). Mussolini sincerely hoped jazz would become the signature music of an Italian Fascist youth movement. Jazz was not Mussolini's own favorite genre—he played and loved classical violin—but he enjoyed it and supported his children's avid interest in it: His daughter Edda was a serious jazz record collector; his son Vittorio started his career writing about jazz before moving to film criticism; and Romano, his youngest son, became an internationally recognized jazz pianist who collaborated late in his career with Duke Ellington, Dizzy Gillespie, and Chet Baker (77–80).

Much of this enthusiasm hinged on a misperception of jazz's origins owing to the success of the ODJB's publicity campaign heralding themselves as the "Creators of Jazz." Italian reprints of the ODJB's Victor and Columbia records and the gramophones they were played on were adduced as evidence of Italian technological modernity and linked in Fascist propaganda to Guglielmo Marconi's invention of the radio. Pride in Nick LaRocca's heritage encouraged some

Italian critics and promoters to inflate his artistic image, casting him as a pioneering jazz *composer*—despite a highly publicized legal case that contravened LaRocca's claim to authorship of "Livery Stable Blues," with the judge stating that the tune was "an old negro melody … that has been known for a great many years" (Leo 2020). Others centered their argument for the ODJB's primacy on the specious claim that the group had introduced improvisation to jazz. In fact, none of the ODJB players were improvisers, at least in the sense in which we now commonly use the term. It is more accurate to say that they were "fakers," the term widely used in early jazz discourse to describe musicians who did not read music and relied instead on their memories of melodies they heard and then replayed. The ODJB themselves called attention to their musical illiteracy with smart-aleck remarks like "I don't know how many pianists we tried before we found one who couldn't read music." As Elijah Wald observes, however, "the ODJB is a perfect example of a band that faked everything but rarely seems to have improvised—each musician presumably worked out his own part, but once he had something he liked, he would play it pretty much the same way from then on" (Wald 2009, 50).[3]

African American musicians did not travel to Italy regularly until the late 1920s, and, as Celenza notes, "there was no 'Harlem' in Rome or Milan, as there was in Paris's Montmartre district" (Celenza 2017, 86). When African American jazz musicians like Louis Armstrong and Sidney Bechet began to arrive in the 1930s, their highly publicized presence, coupled with the growing international influence of French primitivism, led to an acceptance of the idea that authentic jazz was rooted in Black vernacular culture. The idea was reinforced by Hollywood films, which, in part because of Mussolini's love of American cinema, became extremely popular in Italy. "Film brought a face to jazz," Celenza writes, "and in many American films, this face was black" (100). This imagery helped cement in the minds of many Italians the idea that jazz was African American in origin and essence, Nick LaRocca and the ODJB notwithstanding. Nevertheless, *King of Jazz*, the Paul Whiteman vehicle, drew record crowds when it was released in Italy, and Italian audiences were thrilled that the film included performances by Italian American musicians, notably the pioneering jazz violinist Joe Venuti and his collaborator, the guitar virtuoso Eddie Lang (Salvatore Massaro) (Celenza 2017, 103–104).

As in France and Britain, by the early 1930s Italian jazz discourse had become increasingly focused on ostensible racial differences and came with a full repertoire of stereotypes about Black instinct, intuition, irrationality, and sexuality. Anti-jazz screeds came from both the left and the right. Marxist philosopher Antonio Gramsci, in a formulation now more commonly associated with Theodor Adorno's notorious critique of jazz, fretted that "it is inconceivable that the repetition of the Negro's physical gestures as they dance around their fetishes and the constant sound of the syncopated rhythm of jazz bands should have no ideological effects" (Celenza 2017, 88). Italian Fascists who earlier had embraced jazz as a potential cornerstone of Italian national culture reconsidered the idea when the music became increasingly associated with French culture, or with an American culture now figured as annoyingly imperialist. "It is stupid, it is ridiculous, it is anti-Fascist," one such commentator grumbled, "to go into raptures over the belly dances of a mulatto woman [an apparent reference to Josephine Baker] or to run like fools after every American fad that comes over to us from across the ocean" (89).

Mussolini's invasion of Ethiopia in 1935 not only complicated Italy's relationship with the US and the broader international community but also intensified jazz's transatlantic racial politics. The invasion led many Fascist officials to call for a clearer demarcation between "uncivilized" Africans and "civilized" Italians, which translated into an effort to produce a distinctive idiom of Italian jazz shorn of legible Black influences. The Futurists had already been pulling back from assertions made in the early 1920s about the importance of Black culture to the modernist avant-garde. In his 1929 book *Jazz-Band*, Anton Giulio Bragaglia, a Futurist writer and owner of a nightclub in Rome, drew a firm distinction between "Negro jazz" and native Italian dance music and seethed about "animalistic dances" of "colored people" driven by the "epileptic chaos" of jazz syncopation. The Italian composer Alfredo Casella, a staunch champion of jazz, responded by insisting that "jazz has contributed greatly to bringing rhythm back into European music," but the jazz he was keenest to defend was the symphonic style associated with white composers. Casella's narrative of jazz history exactly mirrored the one Paul Whiteman presented in his concerts and his autobiography. "Born in the jungle," Casella wrote, "this art was transformed in the heart and on the lips of the American Negro before it finally reached the North, where it found its ultimate expression in the work of whites, like Whiteman (Christian) or Berlin and Gershwin (Jewish)" (Celenza 2017, 94–99).

These developments pushed the ODJB away from the center of Italian jazz at the same time as the music's stylistic evolution moved the band even further to the margins of American jazz. Italy's invasion of Ethiopia was supported by many pro-Mussolini Italian Americans and roundly condemned by most African Americans, setting the two communities at loggerheads, and unleashing a wave of anti-Italian sentiment across much of the US. This coincided with the beginning of the swing era, when Louis Armstrong and bandleaders like Duke

Ellington, Count Basie, Jimmie Lunceford, Chick Webb, Benny Goodman, and Artie Shaw became not just jazz stars but also Hollywood celebrities. A burgeoning youth culture of swing-record hounds and jitterbug and Lindy Hop dancers received massive publicity in the mainstream media and specialized jazz magazines like *Down Beat* and *Metronome*. An alliance between jazz and leftist politics that had started in the early 1930s intensified with the Popular Front initiatives of the Communist Party after 1935. The person *Harper's* magazine dubbed "Number One Swing Man" was not a musician, but rather the jazz critic, impresario, record producer, and talent scout John Hammond. Hammond, though not a party member, worked with the Harlem branch of the CPUSA to organize union rallies and benefits for civil rights causes that featured Goodman (Hammond's brother-in-law), Ellington, Basie, and other prominent jazz musicians. Hammond used his columns in *Down Beat*, the *Nation*, and the *New Masses* to push for desegregation of the music industry and promote Black performers who "could not get a break because of their race" (Gennari 2006, 34–53).

It was in this fevered context—with its convergence of anti-Italian sentiment, strained relations between African Americans and Italian Americans, the burgeoning alliance between jazz and the political left, and the ODJB's eclipse first by symphonic jazz and then by the swing movement—that Nick LaRocca reemerged into public view with an effort to revive the ODJB and with a series of vitriolic op-ed articles, interviews, and letters disparaging African American musicians and floating conspiracy theories about Communists and Jews.

## V

A primary vehicle for the ODJB's short-lived resurrection in the mid-1930s was a *The March of Time* newsreel in 1937 called "Birth of Swing." *The March of Time*, the newsreel branch of Time, Inc., began in 1935, taking its name from a news documentary series on CBS Radio. *Time*'s editors called the new form's combination of news reporting and dramatic enactments "pictorial journalism"; its immediate success led to Time Inc.'s launching of *Life* magazine. "Birth of Swing" was initiated by the critic J. S. Moynahan (1937), a great admirer of the ODJB, who shaped its storyline around a piece titled "Ragtime to Swing" he had written for the *Saturday Evening Post,* which ran concurrently with the newsreel as it was shown in movie theaters across the US. "Birth of Swing" was entirely based on LaRocca's version of jazz history, summed up with the line "today's swing is only yesterday's jazz, which the Dixieland Band originated in New Orleans twenty years ago." While the reel's documentary aesthetic projected an air of authority and objectivity, its deliberate falsifications and disingenuity turned it into a promotional tool for the ODJB. Hugues Panassié, the French critic shown in the documentary, was the foremost proponent of jazz's essential Blackness and pointedly omitted the ODJB from his very short list of white musicians who could play in the idiom. The newsreel shows footage of such leading swing musicians as Red Norvo, Benny Goodman, Glen Gray, and the drummer and bandleader Chick Webb; Webb is the only Black musician included in the montage, but his face is obscured by one of his cymbals. The newsreel depicts white swing musicians as serious performers of art music—with the ODJB pictured in a tony setting suggestive of a Paul Whiteman-style performance—while showing African American performers as entertainers wearing clownish hats. They perform for the pleasure of an all-white audience, thus representing racial segregation as an accepted fact rather than a social problem ("Birth of Swing"; Dunkel 2021, 214–216).[4]

"Birth of Swing" appeared at a time when debate in the emerging field of US jazz criticism focused on two basic conceptualizations of jazz history: a Marxist-tinged, class-based argument (known as the "white influence school"); and an NAACP-style, race-based argument (the "colored influence school"). The two arguments were not mutually exclusive, and influential critics like Hammond shifted between them. The foremost proponent of the first was Charles Edward Smith, who defined authentic jazz as a Southern, interracial, multiethnic, proletarian folk music. Smith wrote a column for *Esquire*, "Collecting Hot," aimed at the fast-growing community of jazz aficionados who combed Salvation Army stores and attics looking for out-of-print discs. Smith treasured his own vintage copies of the early ODJB records, and when he set out to write a column about the band, he wrote to LaRocca asking for a photograph. Smith wanted to make the case for the ODJB's seminal role in hot jazz. That role, as Smith saw it, was to assimilate Black folk music and present a version of it that was accessible to white musicians such as the trumpeter Bix Beiderbecke, who critics then and now esteem as the most important white player of the 1920s. Even in the view of an avowed fan and sympathetic critic like Smith, LaRocca's role was as a mere conduit between an authentic Black musical language and its superior white interpreters. LaRocca, insulted, rebuffed Smith (Dunkel 2021, 192–198, 205–209).

In one respect the *March of Time* newsreel *did* frame the ODJB in a way that aligned with Smith's model. For Smith, jazz's generative force had less to do with the virtuosity of individual musicians than it did with what he called the "welding" of different traditions of folk music. Smith's welding concept was a way of bringing ethnicity together with class while resisting the problematic metaphor of the melting pot; welding melts the edges of two pieces but otherwise leaves them largely intact. This fits nicely into the larger discourse of the major social movements of the 1930s American Left that Michael Denning has characterized as the "cultural front"—the leftist vision of ethnic pluralism and class solidarity expressed in a wealth of literature, visual art, and music of the period (Denning 1996; Dunkel, 2021, 198).

The ODJB represented the multiethnic, proletarian roots of New Orleans jazz—the musicians came from families rooted in generations of manual labor, and they retained their working-class identities even while accessing spaces of middle-class and aristocratic leisure in Manhattan and London. Back when the ODJB had their New York debut in 1917, when the band members arrived at the Reisenweber Cafe for the first time, the room in which they were to perform was pitch dark: The lights were not working. Both LaRocca and trombonist Daddy Edwards were licensed electricians who had honed their musical skills during breaks from their electrical work in New Orleans. After helping Sbarbaro carry his drums to the bandstand in the dark, they went to the basement of the building, found the fuse box, and fixed the improperly installed wiring, bringing light to the bandstand and dance floor (Bomberger 2018, 31–32).

There is a sequence in the *March of Time* newsreel where LaRocca reassembles the ODJB by pulling each musician out of their ordinary jobs at a YMCA, a Bible House, a radio station, and a car-repair shop. Sbarbaro reportedly protested the producers' original plan to cast him as a kitchen assistant, only agreeing to be filmed when they instead made him an auto mechanic. An auto mechanic/drummer and front-line men who were handy with a toolbox—here was an image fully in sync with the Common Man discourse of the New Deal and the concomitant masculinized jazz discourse of the period.

Concurrent with the ODJB's return to public view was the beginning of Nick LaRocca's bitter war of words against the jazz critical establishment, a skirmish that was shadowed by stark class dynamics. LaRocca's main antagonist was Marshall Stearns, scion of a Boston Brahmin family, a scholar of medieval English just then starting a more consequential career as a jazz proselytizer. Later Stearns would be the founder of the Institute of Jazz Studies, play a key role in the State Department's jazz diplomacy program in the 1950s, and publish two very important books, *The Story of Jazz* (1956) and (with his wife Jean) *Jazz Dance* (1964). Like John Hammond, Stearns was a staunch antiracist and civil rights activist. When teaching at Indiana University in the mid-1940s, he helped establish the campus's NAACP chapter after a series of racist incidents. While studying for his doctorate at Yale, Stearns started a column in *Down Beat* called "The History of Swing," the first history of jazz written by an American that was unequivocal about the primary role of Black musicians at every stage of the music's evolution. The column ran from 1936 to 1938, a time when *Down Beat* was dominated by coverage of white musicians. The magazine received letters from readers claiming that Stearns overstated anti-Black racism and was biased against whites (Gennari 2006, 144–155; Dunkel 2021, 313–349).

LaRocca responded to the first installment of Stearns's column with a letter angrily accusing Stearns of trying to "discredit the Original Dixieland Jazz Band the Originators of the Jazz or Swing Style of Music The First Jazz Band in the World." LaRocca's sketchy typography and orthography underscored the class difference between an Italian American musician from an immigrant working-class family and an Ivy League PhD student from a well-healed Boston WASP one. *Down Beat* hesitated to print LaRocca's letter in full, instead allowing Stearns to use excerpts from it in another of his columns, "Questions and Low Down on the Hot Men" (1936), where he answered questions from readers. Over the course of multiple columns, Stearns toned down his critique of the ODJB but held firm to his view that the band was artistically insignificant to the development of jazz. In a personal letter to LaRocca in 1937, Stearns told him that he (LaRocca) had "failed to give colored musicians a break; and that is why I exaggerated the other extreme, since the public is inclined to believe you and musicians of your opinion." But Stearns directly challenged LaRocca's assertion that he was uninfluenced by Black musicians, citing the African American trombonist and writer Preston Jackson as saying he saw LaRocca "and the rest of the boys who later formed the Original Dixieland Jazz Band come in often to listen to King Oliver and his band." Deeply wounded by the denial of his paternity by jazz critics and historians, LaRocca suffered what felt to him the worst form of abjection: to be dethroned as "the first man of jazz" by Black men, and worse, for the dethroning to be carried out by supercilious white men (LaRocca 1936a, 1936b, 1936c; Stearns 1936, 1937; Dunkel 2021, 212–215).

Years later, LaRocca wrote to Mississippi Senator James Eastland, a notorious segregationist, asking him to investigate the "propaganda" regarding New Orleans jazz history "compiled by the northern carpetbaggers" like the "Jew" Marshall Stearns. "These people control the press because of their position in the social world," LaRocca fumed. "This jazz movement is nothing but to bring on integration between the poor white man and the colored race, as these parasites are already segregated from their own poor white people." This letter is one of several in the Hogan archive that reveal the deep class consciousness underlying LaRocca's bitterness, an attitude that aligns with what historians have taught us about the cultural and political populism of poor southern whites, the vulnerable class that bolstered the white supremacist Democratic machine that dominated New Orleans politics from the 1890s to the middle of the twentieth century. Dixieland was "an expression of this group's identity and pride," Burton Peretti (1994) has argued. For Italians, who were in a precarious and paradoxical position as victims of lynching and other forms of racial violence while also being key contributors to the white political coalition, Dixieland may have been especially important as a space of cultural belonging and psychological safety. LaRocca resented members of the WASP ruling class who treated him "like a poor dago boy on the other side of the tracks" when he returned to New Orleans in 1925, just a few years after he performed for the Queen of England. He could not understand how anyone could fault him for feeling he owed nothing to African Americans. "Not having associated with 'em, not knowing 'em," he said in one interview, "how was I to give these colored men a break? I couldn't even give myself a break. I had to make that break" (LaRocca 1936a, WHRA interviews).

## VI

Despite a brief uptick of interest following the *March of Time* newsreel and the release of new recordings of the band's best-known tunes, the Nick LaRocca-led ODJB receded to the margins once again. When Benny Goodman performed a radio version of his "Twenty Years of Jazz" Carnegie Hall concert in 1938, he invited Sbarbaro, Edwards, and Shields to perform with his band, and in *The Kingdom of Swing*, his 1939 autobiography, Goodman praises Shields as one of his key influences on the clarinet (Brunn 1960, 201–205). H. O. Brunn makes a great deal of this in his charming but breathtakingly hagiographic book *The Story of the Original Dixieland Jazz Band*, anointing Goodman as the next great figure in jazz history after—yes—Shields and LaRocca. Published in 1960, Brunn's book is almost entirely bereft of African American musicians. It ends on an elegiac note, with LaRocca, who would die the next year, living "in a two-story house of his own construction at 2218 Constance Street in New Orleans, in the same neighborhood that in 1897 heard the baleful sounds of his cornet" (253).

More than six decades later, LaRocca and the ODJB continue to occupy a vexed position in jazz history. In 2017, the centennial of their seminal recording received notice in several important quarters, including the US Library of Congress. The Recorded Sound Division of the LOC posted a webpage that recounted the circumstances of the recording date and offered a measured assessment of its significance, concluding that "while novelty-imbued and raucous," the ODJB played music that was "deliberate, rehearsed, and well-executed. And, whereas the ODJB did not invent jazz, nor were they the first to introduce it up north, they did create it for the first time ever on a phonograph record, one-hundred years ago" (Cornell 2017). Striking a different note, *The Irish Times* marked the occasion with an article making the tendentious assertion that the ODJB were "the victim of an inverse racism" who had been falsely accused of "pirating and vulgarising black music." Allowing that "black music and rhythm were of course fundamental to the creation of jazz," the *Times* writer observed that jazz "was also a hybrid of marching band and Irish music as well as opera" (Norris 2017).

The evaluation of the ODJB's significance rendered some ninety years ago by Charles Edward Smith and Marshall Stearns largely has not been challenged or contradicted in the work of subsequent generations of jazz critics and historians. Typical of recent historiography is Ted Gioia's account in *The History of Jazz*, where he affirms the long-standing post-1930s consensus that African American musicians like King Oliver, Freddie Keppard, Jelly Roll Morton, Sidney Bechet, and, of course, Louis Armstrong were by far the more consequential figures in the music's development, while also defending the ODJB against "smug dismissals." Gioia praises LaRocca's playing as "supple and often inspired" and assents to the view that Larry Shields had a significant influence on Benny Goodman and other musicians of the 1930s and '40s. "[F]ew bands of that period," Gioia concludes, "did more to expose the wider public, at home and abroad, to the virtues of this new music from New Orleans" (Gioia 1997, 38–39). I know of no reputable academic or journalistic account of jazz claiming to be a comprehensive cultural history that does not tell the story of the ODJB's early recordings, their triumphant tour of England, and their influence on other white musicians.

The most acute reckoning with the ODJB and its legacy occurs at the intersection of jazz studies and Italian American studies. In line with historical and cultural studies more generally, these fields have become increasingly concerned with issues of canonicity and cultural memory, scrutinizing how the histories of art forms or of group experiences are constructed, represented, circulated, and interpreted. Which jazz performers and performances are the ones chosen to represent a large and multifarious history of playing and listening? Of the millions who share an ethnic heritage, which people, places, and events are chosen to represent that group's history and experience? What are the platforms and venues, the rhetorical tools and strategies, by which such selections become exemplary and archetypical?

In such macro-level investigation, the issue of *invention*, and more broadly of origins and primacy, is especially fraught. For artistic canons and group histories to perform work as popular narratives—as legible and appealing stories—it helps enormously to be able to identify an unambiguous beginning, an agreed-upon point of origin and departure. While academic historians and cultural theorists delight in "problematizing" any kind of clean consensus about how ideas, forms, and experiences begin and take shape over time, popular narratives generally employ a mode of storytelling that minimizes focus on conflicting and multiple interpretations. The goal is decidedly *not* to present case studies in critical analysis or theoretical debate, but rather to present an orderly, uncluttered, smoothly contoured story.

The notion that Nick LaRocca and the ODJB invented jazz is plainly preposterous on its face. But so too is the notion that any individual musician or ensemble invented jazz. Among jazz historians, there is not even agreement that New Orleans should be heralded as the "birthplace" of jazz. As heretical (and preposterous) as it would be not to center New Orleans in early jazz history, positing a single place of origin for an artistic form and practice as far-reaching and multifarious as jazz ignores or defies the complexity, messiness, and indeterminacy of artistic creativity and cultural circulation almost as much as the single-inventor theory (Johnson 2020, 131–133).

The case is further complicated by ethnic politics. When I first presented this material at a symposium held at Tulane University, the folklorist and Italian American studies scholar Joseph Sciorra, in a thoughtful response, diagnosed the Nick LaRocca case as an example of "what historian Robert Fleegler calls the 'contributionism' paradigm in which white ethnics flaunt their so-called 'gifts to the nation' regardless how tainted, to assuage a lingering group inferiority complex." Sciorra reminds us that LaRocca and his supporters anointed him the "Christopher Columbus of Music"; like the infamous world explorer from Genoa, he is "a particularly disquieting and distasteful figure within Italian American discourse," yet there are some Italian Americans "who unequivocally embrace and celebrate such a historical figure in the present moment" (Sciorra 2022). Sciorra and fellow Italian American studies scholar Laura Ruberto have collaborated to produce deeply researched and incisive scholarship examining the history and politics of Columbus Day celebrations and Columbus public statuary and place names. Their work offers scrupulously even-handed accounts of the circumstances that led to efforts by Italian American *prominenti* to establish Columbus as the group's preeminent symbol; the irony of a largely peasant and working-class population of Italian immigrants and their American progeny being represented archetypically by a monarchically financed proto-capitalist; the understandable desire of contemporary Italian Americans to be included in the culture of US public memorialization and celebration; and powerful social justice claims and efforts to correct the historical record on the part of US indigenous peoples and their supporters (Ruberto and Sciorra 2020).

We are confronted with the fact that two iconic figures of Italian and Italian American achievement have been, in one case, a man who initiated the colonization and exploitation of the Americas and unleashed genocidal violence against its indigenous populations, and in a second case, a man who sullied his own notable achievements by proudly trumpeting racist and arch-segregationist views. Of course, the difference in the scale of mischief here is profound, and we risk trivializing Columbus's epochal impact by likening it to that of an unexceptional musical entertainer/construction worker. But one does perceive here an unmistakable formula for Italian American canonization, begging an important question: Is there something intrinsic to Italian America, something hard-wired into the DNA of its history, sociology, politics, economics, and culture, such that the accomplishments it chooses to celebrate are those that come at the expense of groups positioned lower in the American racial hierarchy? Put another way: Is the formula for Italian American success fundamentally and exclusively a process of securing and wielding white power?

Sciorra forensically distills the matter: "How does one properly position, discuss, and confront the 'first jazz recording' within Italian American history and culture, and US history more generally, given the Original Dixieland Jazz Band's white privilege and LaRocca's blatant racism without falling into the trap of one-dimensional ethnic boosterism, and even more troubling, using Italian ethnicity and expressivity as a cover for whiteness and veiled white supremacy?" (Sciorra 2022)

One surefire way to fall into the trap Sciorra warns against is to entrust the commemoration of the ODJB to a local ethnic booster who is an avowed neo-Confederate. This has been the case in New Orleans, where a plaque memorializing LaRocca adorns the corner of Esplanade and Decatur Streets, in front of the US Mint Building. Oddly, though it carries the title "Sicilian Jazz," the plaque is focused almost entirely on LaRocca, attributing the ODJB's accomplishments singularly to LaRocca, noting that his composition "Tiger Rag" has become a favorite of LSU football fans, and crediting him (along with Louis Prima) in being "instrumental in introducing swing music." The plaque was commissioned by Charles Marsala, a Sicilian-American businessman who sits on the city's monument advisory committee. According to an account published by the Music and Cultural Coalition of New Orleans (which has opposed the plaque), Marsala has courted controversy on that committee by advocating preservation of Confederate monuments, describing those who advocate their demolition or removal from civic space as "Marxists" and "Antifa." Marsala has been heard to tout

Confederate leaders as benefactors of African Americans—claiming, for instance, that Jefferson Davis "empowered" his slaves through education. The "Sicilian Jazz" plaque is silent about LaRocca's social views, but given Marsala's perspective as a self-described amateur historian, it would not be surprising if the plaque were to herald LaRocca's segregationist position as a boon to African Americans (MCCNO 2020).

The ODJB richly deserves recognition for its place in jazz history, as does LaRocca himself. But if the point is to memorialize "Sicilian Jazz" in New Orleans, individuals other than LaRocca could serve as far less controversial standard bearers. In fact, the city has already embraced this challenge by designating the site of the J&M Recording Studio as a historical landmark. J&M was the place where record producer Cosimo Matassa engineered the "New Orleans sound" of 1950s and '60s rhythm and blues and rock 'n' roll in his work with Little Richard, Fats Domino, Big Joe Turner, Aaron Neville, and other local (but soon to become internationally famous) Black musicians. As George De Stefano has shown in his important work on Sicilian New Orleans, Matassa was well-known for personal warmth, a spirit of mutual respect, and an inclusive, collaborative ethos that crossed the color line at a time of acute racial unrest and upheaval. Here is a far more appealing image of the social life and civic contribution of Italian Americans—a model for Italian American success predicated not on the assertion of white privilege, but something more like its principled relinquishment (De Stefano 2019, 74–78).

Jazz scholars have provided ample means with which to both honor and critically analyze the ODJB as well as the Sicilian and Italian musical culture in New Orleans from the late nineteenth century to the present. I would again urge attention to the exemplary work of Bruce Boyd Raeburn. What I especially admire and recommend is how Raeburn conceives of New Orleans musical culture as a heterogenous and multivalent soundscape even while excavating and mapping the careers of individual musicians across lines of race and ethnicity. In taking this approach, he helps us understand music as a social network and a cultural *process*, one that cannot be fully (or even best) captured by focusing only on those musicians who build successful public careers and enjoy the privilege of being spotlighted for their individual achievements. In a salient example of this brand of "beyond the canon" jazz history, Raeburn traces the pattern of musical education in late-nineteenth-century New Orleans, pinpointing the consequential role played by Italian music teachers in both Italian and African American neighborhoods and schools (Raeburn 2009, 142–149)

The project of assessing and memorializing the ODJB continues to unfold in a transatlantic context. In 2015, a film titled *Sicily Jass: The World's First Man in Jazz* was released in Italy. Written and directed by Rome-based multimedia artist Michele Cinque, the film adopts a heavily elegiac tone to convey the meaning of Nick LaRocca's career and legacy. To an American sensibility, the film is a rather odd artifact. Its mélange of documentary-styled presentation, talking-head interviews, and dramatizations by the renowned *contastorie* (storyteller) Mimmo Cuticchio, a master of the island's venerable tradition of marionette theater, situates the film in an ambiguous space between positivist history and expressive aestheticism. LaRocca is claimed by his family's ancestral village of Salaparuta while also being projected into a fantastical New Orleans whose history is twisted and sharply foreshortened. The film proposes to sustain the myth announced in its title while also casting LaRocca as mistreated, misunderstood, and ultimately forgotten. Cinque shapes a defensive posture toward LaRocca's racism; one of his interviewees goes so far as to claim that LaRocca was "driven to" his bigotry by bad-faith critics and journalists. In an awkward and truncated effort to address the issue of jazz's racial provenance, a disconcertingly out-of-context clip of the renowned African American poet and jazz critic Amiri Baraka asserting that jazz is fundamentally Black is shoehorned into a narrative that otherwise makes no effort to document African American culture (Lomanno 2019).

Despite these shortcomings, *Sicily Jass* projects an undeniable beauty. This owes largely to a lush visual palimpsest evoking Sicilian pastoralism and archaism, especially in haunting images of the island's architectural ruins. These scenes come bathed in a poignant original score by Salvatore Bonafede, set off by a passage in which the phrase "and yet silence becomes music" deftly enfolds the film's soundscape into its mise-en-scène.

I am struck by a deep irony here. As I observed earlier when drawing on Anna Harwell Celenza's (2017) account of jazz in Italy in the interwar period, the basis on which Italian Fascist cultural ideologues embraced the music was its singular modernity, its affiliation with new technologies, its aesthetic progressivism, its orientation toward a triumphal, affluent future. Italy was no longer to be pigeonholed as a vessel of a soft, feminine aestheticism, supplicant to the virile, masculine Northern European imperial powers. It would link itself to America at that country's moment of international ascendence and growing strength buttressed by military prowess, industrial might, dynamic urbanism, and the ever-burgeoning power of its culture industries.

As we have seen, Italian jazz's own developing ecosystem centered itself in northern urban centers among social elites. Mussolini himself personally enjoyed and had a strong familial connection to jazz. The Fascist leader's passion for the arts and catholic musical tastes came with one glaring exception: He strongly disliked Southern Italian folk music and was especially dismissive of the local styles of Naples and Sicily, regarding such music as hopelessly sentimental and nostalgic—backward, that is, hence not fit for a national culture that was moving energetically and inexorably forward. As ever, Italian culture and politics were shadowed by—even constituted by—a palpable north/south dynamic. Those Fascists whose valorization of jazz was in some part connected to the ODJB's moment of international fame did not make a point of emphasizing LaRocca's Sicilian heritage—even though, in 1919, the Italian consul to New Orleans had written a letter boasting about the role played by Italian immigrants (most of them Sicilian) in the development of jazz (Celenza 2017, 7–8).

More than a century later, Italy can boast of a vibrant and internationally significant jazz culture, with world-renowned festivals, clubs, record labels, academic journals, magazines, conferences, and educational programs. While much of this ecosystem is centered in the North—notably the Umbria Jazz Festival in Perugia and recording companies and publicity organs in Milan and Rome—several of Italy's most highly regarded jazz musicians, including the superb saxophonist Francesco Cafiso, come from Sicily. Not one of them is mentioned in *Sicily Jass*. Indeed, the film might lead one to conclude that there really has never been a jazz culture in Sicily—just a distant, happenstance connection to a musician with a highly dubious claim to being "the world's first man of jazz." A man, a fine musician, who deserves a place in jazz history. A flawed man whose flagrant bigotry complicates that claim. A man who, when taken on as a subject by an earnest filmmaker/hagiographer, finds his memory—perhaps fittingly, perhaps not—lying in a land of ruins.

## VII

Here are two twentieth-century inventions that have not aged well: Fascism and Dixieland jazz. Granted, the scope, scale, and human consequences of their respective downsides makes the coupling of these two things a bit nutty: on one side, jackbooted thugs, authoritarianism, martial law, eugenics, genocide; on the other, boozed-up, straw-hatted white men evoking the good-time Old South in rousing choruses of "When the Saints Go Marching In."

In the years just after World War II, with the Western world recovering from the horrors unleashed by Mussolini and Hitler, the birth of what became known as the Dixieland Revival sparked a sectarian war in the jazz world. Dixieland partisans built their case for the superiority of the idiom in part on its putative anti-Fascist qualities. Proudly calling themselves "moldy figs," they argued that the earlier music evinced qualities of warmth, intimacy, and soulfulness that had disappeared in the cacophony of mechanistic big bands and the cool, detached, affectless posture of the beboppers. Swing orchestras were portrayed as militaristic, totalitarian bureaucracies led by cult-of-personality celebrity bandleaders who dominated and infantilized their audiences. Bebop was an insidious conspiracy propagated by enemy-of-the-people pseudo-intellectuals. The so-called "progressive jazz" movement was led by marquee bandleader Stan Kenton, an Ayn Rand-inspired, self-styled jazz businessman-superhero who wrote cold, bombastic orchestral works seemingly glorifying American superpower in the atomic age. Against these fascistic travesties, traditional jazz—or simply *jazz* for the figs, who regarded the modern styles as apostasy against the real article—stood for honesty, authenticity, artisanship, homespun democracy, and human-scale sociality.

We presently witness the resurrection of fascism, as evidenced in the person and the movement associated with Donald Trump; in the election in Italy in 2022 of a neofascist female prime minister; in a persistently divisive politics of immigration, citizenship, and civil rights driven by the widespread ascendance of white nationalism. It may or may not be coincidental that Dixieland and other strains of musical Americana also have been undergoing revival in recent years. I am not thinking of your grandfather's "businessman's bounce," or of the long-term, steady popularity of small-group collective polyphony in brisk 2/4 time played across the world, absent the racial baggage such music shoulders in its nation of origin. I am thinking of acts like one from my neck of the woods, Vermont Joy Parade, a six-piece ensemble of banjo, trumpet, accordion, guitar, upright bass, and percussion playing an eclectic blend of Dixieland, country blues and old-time string tunes, Cajun, polka, klezmer, and jug music. Dubbing itself a pioneer of "suspender fusion," the group (now disbanded, unfortunately) sported a pose of loose trousered, mustachioed Americana hipsterism while projecting an antic vibe redolent of old-fashioned circus and vaudeville sideshows.

I am thinking of the old-time string band the Carolina Chocolate Drops, its breakout star Rhiannon Giddens, and other African American musicians who have undertaken the excavation of post-1830s American music born of plantation cabins, minstrel shows, barn raisings, square dances, hootenannies, agricultural fairs, railroad laborer Gandy dancing, rodeos, and the like, insisting on the Black and interracial roots of this wide range of vernacular cultural expression. This pining for roots, the rural, and the old-timey cuts against deeply worn grooves in the racial coding of American music. Like the styles labeled "country" and "classic rock," Dixieland came to be categorized as white music despite its origins in Black and interracial culture. Such is the fundamental racial dialectic of American popular culture: When younger African American musicians and audiences carve out a space of innovation and creative leadership (blues, swing, bebop, R&B, soul, funk, hip-hop) that becomes recognized as the cutting-edge of American popular music writ large, large swaths of the white population gravitate to older styles. It is not just the sound of the new music that fractures the audience; it is the larger cultural atmosphere and landscape shaped and signified by the music. Music connected with urban life, the body, and transgression is pigeonholed as "Black." Music connected with small town, rural, and suburban life, nostalgia, and safety registers in the popular imagination as "white."

Phyllis Rose has argued that the two "most important movements of mind in the twentieth century" centered on race (Rose 1991, 36). Nazism, adjacent fascist movements, and Jim Crow were driven by a quest for racial purity, a permanent system of segregation and social hierarchy confirming and upholding the superiority of one group. In the aesthetic and social energies associated with jazz and related developments in the realms of modern literature, arts, and civic life, the central thrust was miscegenation, cultural cross-breeding, the frisson of difference, and a recognition that certain people otherwise considered inferior might, owing to the richness of their inherited culture, possess superior aesthetic intuitions and abilities.

These movements have not been mutually exclusive, and neither one has been a model of consistency, logic, and cogency. Jazz was not only compatible with Italian Fascism; it was a central plank of Mussolini's cultural program, and his own son became an accomplished figure in the music. More than a few Nazi officials secretly built jazz record collections; party social events sometimes featured swing dancing to the music of Black and Jewish bandleaders. Even as Dixieland increasingly tilted toward whiteness, many of its adherents imputed anti-Fascist qualities to the music. On the other hand, notwithstanding perennial efforts to proselytize jazz as a space where "cats of any color" can thrive, that space has never completely overcome racialized patterns, and no small amount of structural racism, in its own business practices, programming strategies, educational programs, and organs of publicity, criticism, and historiography.

Jazz is large and full of dissonances and incongruities; it contains multitudes. So too does Italian American history and culture. Nick LaRocca was not the only racist jazz musician, and the ODJB was not the only jazz group that profited from racial privilege. Many Italian American jazz musicians—the list is long but let me single out, in recent decades, Chuck and Gap Mangione, Gene Perla, Joe Lovano, and Joey DeFrancesco—have been well-known for their fruitful collaborations and mutually respectful relations with African American colleagues. The ODJB, because of the unique space it inhabits in the histories of both jazz and Italian America, nevertheless deserves special scrutiny. LaRocca and the ODJB are important to jazz history and Italian American history not just because they happened to make the first commercial jazz phonograph record, and not just because LaRocca was an ignominious figure; they are important, rather, because their story illuminates a set of issues hovering at the intersection of Italian immigration, colonialism, racialization, modernism, and Fascism. Reckoning with the specific racial dynamics that shaped where and how the ODJB performed, how they were received, and how they have been remembered—and doing so in a transatlantic framework that foregrounds Italy and Italian America—is vital if we are to convey just how large and multitudinous is that space where jazz studies, Italian American studies, and diasporic Italian studies intersect.

## Notes

[1] Raeburn (2009) touches on the discrimination experienced by New Orleans-based Arbreshe musicians. The Arbreshe were Italo-Albanians, some of whom settled in Sicily and became part of the Sicilian emigration to the Gulf Coast South.

[2] My discussion in this section draws heavily on Mario Dunkel's (2021) brilliant analysis of Whiteman in *The Stories of Jazz*.

[3] The exception was drummer Tony Sbarbaro. Sbarbaro deserves more attention that I can give him in this paper. As drum-kit historian Matt Brennan had observed, Sbarbaro played a significant role in the history of his instrument. Alone among his bandmates, Sbarbaro was a skillful improviser. He had a flamboyant style featuring clever mixing of flams, rolls, and other drum rudiments with a pioneering approach to the drum kit as such, using cowbells, woodblocks, and cymbals in addition to drum skins. His propulsive rhythms were key to the ODJB's exciting impact.

[4] Here too I am deeply indebted to Dunkel's (2021) analysis.

## Works Cited

Bebco, Joe. 2019. "Reconsidering Dixieland Jazz: How the Name Has Harmed the Music." The Syncopated Times. January 27. https://syncopatedtimes.com/reconsidering-dixieland-jazz/ (accessed January 21, 2023).

"Birth of Swing." 1937. *March of Time*. Columbia Broadcasting Service. https://www.youtube.com/watch?v=UHZIsfJ-m8U (accessed January 22, 2023).

Bomberger, E. Douglas. 2018. *Making Music American: 1917 and the Transformation of Culture*. New York: Oxford University Press.

Boulard, Garry. 1988. "Blacks, Italians, and the Making of New Orleans Jazz." *Journal of Ethnic Studies* 16/1: 53–66.

Brunn, H. O. 1960. *The Story of the Original Dixieland Jazz Band*. Baton Rouge: Louisiana University Press.

Carney, Court. 2009. *Cuttin' Up: How Early Jazz Got America's Ear*. 2009. Lawrence: University Press of Kansas.

Celenza, Anna Harwell. 2017. *Jazz Italian Style: From Its Origins in New Orleans to Fascist Italy and Sinatra*. New York: Cambridge University Press.

Charters, Samuel. 2008. *A Trumpet Around the Corner: The Story of New Orleans Jazz*. Jackson: University Press of Mississippi.

Cornell, Bryan. 2017. "The First Jazz Recording: One Hundred Years Later." https://blogs.loc.gov/now-see-hear/2017/03/the-first-jazz-recording-one-hundred-years-later (accessed January 21, 2023).

Denning, Michael. 1996. *The Cultural Front: The Laboring of American Culture in the Twentieth Century*. New York: Verso.

De Stefano, George. 2019. "Sonic Affinities: Sicilian and African American Musical Encounters in New Orleans." *Italian American Review* 9/1: 68–88.

Dunkel, Mario. 2021. *The Stories of Jazz: Narrating a Musical Tradition*. Vienna: Hollitzer Verlag.

Gennari, John. 2006. *Blowin' Hot and Cool: Jazz and Its Critics*. Chicago: University of Chicago Press.

Gennari, John. 2017. *Flavor and Soul: Italian America at Its African American Edge*. Chicago: University of Chicago Press.

Gioia, Ted. 1997. *The History of Jazz*. New York: Oxford University Press.

Gushee, Lawrence. 2010. *Pioneers of Jazz: The Story of the Creole Band*. New York: Oxford University Press.

Hersch, Charles. 2007. *Subversive Sounds: Race and the Birth of Jazz in New Orleans*. Chicago: University of Chicago Press.

Johnson, Bruce. 2020. *Jazz Diaspora: Music and Globalisation*. New York: Routledge.

Lane, Jeremy. 2013. *Jazz and Machine-Age Imperialism: Music, 'Race,' and Intellectuals in France, 1918–1945*. Ann Arbor: University of Michigan Press.

LaRocca, Dominic James "Nick." Interviews recorded for William Ransom Hogan Archive of New Orleans Jazz (WRHA), Tulane University (May 26, 1958; June 2, 1958; June 9, 1958; October 26, 1959).

LaRocca, Dominic James "Nick." 1936a. Letter to Marshall Stearns (June 17, 1936). WRHA.

LaRocca, Dominic James "Nick." 1936b. Letter to Marshall Stearns (August 12, 1936). WRHA.

LaRocca, Dominic James "Nick." 1936c. "LaRocca Takes Swing Critic for a Ride." *Down Beat* 3 (September 1936), 6.

Leo, Katherine. 2018. "The ODJB at 100: Revisiting Essential Narratives and Copyright Control of Victor 18255. *Jazz @100*. Darmstadt Studies in Jazz Research 15. Edited by Wolfgang Knauer.

Leo, Katherine. 2020. "Early Blues and Jazz Authorship in the Case of the 'Livery Stable Blues.'" *Jazz Perspectives* 3/3: 311–338.

Lomanno, Mark. 2019. "'Stay with It All the Way Down': Michele Cinque Recounts Nick LaRocca's Incurable Wounds." *Italian American Review* 9/1: 135–140.

Moynahan, James H. S. 1937. "Ragtime to Swing." *Saturday Evening Post* (February 13): 14–15, 40, 42, 44.

Music and Cultural Coalition of New Orleans (MCCNO). 2020. "How a New Historic Marker Creates a Literal Link to White Supremacy in the French Quarter." *Antigravity Magazine*. https://antigravitymagazine.com/column/how-a-historic-marker-and-attached-qr-code-create-a-literal-link-to-white-supremacy-in-the-french-quarter/.

Norris, David. 2017. "Remembering the Real 'Inventors of Jazz.'" *The Irish Times*, July 8, 2017. https://www.irishtimes.com/culture/music/remembering-the-real-inventors-of-jazz-1.3144305 (accessed January 21, 2023).

Peretti, Burton. 1994. *The Creation of Jazz: Music, Race, and Culture in Urban America*. Urbana Champaign: University of Illinois Press.

Raeburn, Bruce Boyd. 2009. "Stars of David and Sons of Italy: Constellations Beyond the Canon in Early New Orleans Jazz." *Jazz Perspectives* 3/2: 123–152.

Raeburn, Bruce Boyd. 2014. "Italian Americans in Early Jazz: Bel Canto Meets the Funk." *Italian American Review* 4/2: 87–108.

Rose, Phyllis. 1991. *Jazz Cleopatra: Josephine Baker in Her Own Time*. New York: Vintage.

Ruberto, Laura E. and Joseph Sciorra. 2020. "Toppling Columbus, Recasting Italian Americans." *Process: A Blog for American History*. https://www.processhistory.org/rubertosciorra-toppling-columbus/?

Sciorra, Joseph. 2022. Respondent to John Gennari at "The Italian Immigrant Experience: Between Black and White" symposium, September 24, Tulane University, New Orleans.

Stearns, Marshall. 1936. "Questions and Low Down on the Hot Men." *Down Beat* 3 (August 1936): 4.

Stearns, Marshall. 1937. Letter to Nick LaRocca (January 11). WRHA.

Sudhalter, Richard. 2001. *Lost Chords: White Musicians and Their Contributions to Jazz, 1915–1945*. New York: Oxford University Press.

Wald, Elijah. 2009. *How the Beatles Destroyed Rock 'N' Roll: An Alternative History of American Popular Music*. New York: Oxford University Press.

Whiteman, Paul (with Mary Margaret McBride). 1926. *Jazz*. New York: J. H. Sears and Company.

# Italian Americans, Confederate Whiteness, and Commemorative Landscapes in New Orleans and Beyond: A Reply to John Gennari's 2022 Tulane University Keynote

JOSEPH SCIORRA

John Gennari's expansive account situates the troublesome Original Dixieland Jazz Band at the confluence of music, race, class, and migration in New Orleans and the United States with particular attention to transnational influences and concerns.[1] His eloquent and informative reading of the historical record is grounded in exploring aspects of Italian American cultural practices and representation, as the 2022 Tulane University symposium subtitle states, "between white and black." Gennari demonstrates unambiguously how the band members' whiteness privileged them in getting gigs, especially in high-end venues—not only in Jim Crow America but also in Europe—in recordings, and perhaps most notably in their placement in the early written histories of jazz that were all routinely and systematically closed to African Americans.

Gennari rightly addresses band leader Nick LaRocca's disturbing and vile statements as he sought to purge African Americans from the development and innovation of this Black American art form and, more specifically, his racist disparagements of African Americans in general. LaRocca, a self-avowed segregationist and the "Christopher Columbus of Music," as he dubbed himself, is a particularly disquieting and distasteful figure within Italian American discourse. Yet some unequivocally embrace and continue to celebrate such a figure. This uncritical treatment follows what historian Robert Fleegler calls the "contributionism" paradigm in which white ethnics flaunt their so-called "gifts to the nation," often at the exclusion of people of color, regardless of how compromised, to assuage a lingering group-inferiority complex (Fleeger 2013, 12–16; see also Harvey 1993, 1–27).

Gennari's narrated journey through the twentieth century and into the present day is attentive to historically specific contexts and variegated media representations—a worthwhile perspective for examining current iterations of Italian Americans' white identity politics. His discerning keynote and now published article demands that we consider how to properly position, discuss, and confront the "first jazz recording" within Italian American history and culture, and US history more broadly, given the Original Dixieland Jazz Band's white privilege and LaRocca's blatant racism. Gennari's intervention challenges us to be leery of one-dimensional ethnic boosterism especially when it serves as a cover for white supremacy.

An illuminating site for examining such matters is found at the corner of Esplanade Avenue and Decatur Street, at the edge of New Orleans's French Quarter and Marigny neighborhoods. There, on the grounds of the Old US Mint building, stands a brown-and-gold metal historical marker inaugurated in 2020 that reads:

> ### SICILIAN JAZZ
> In December 1915, Nick LaRocca was playing Jass music at Canal St. & St. Charles Ave. to promote a World Championship fight. He was asked to play in Chicago. From Chicago, he went to New York and recorded music titled "Jass." LaRocca decided to change the name on future albums to "Jazz." His first recording "Livery Stable Blues" sold over 1,000,000 copies. His later song "Tiger Rag" is a favorite of LSU fans. Louis Prima followed LaRocca in 1934 and was instrumental in introducing swing music.

The sign's inscription further states that it was "Sponsored by the Marsala Cultural Fund" and encourages those interested "to learn more" by visiting a website and to scan a QR code for a tour of "Little Palermo" (i.e., the French Quarter).[2]

I am not concerned here with the accuracy of this commemorative placard—Gennari's analysis provides us with all the tools needed to unpack the embossed statement—but I am instead interested in how such a memorializing initiative reveals the confluence of contemporary Italian ethnicity, white grievance about perceived disempowerment, and public spaces.[3] The sign's placement is not limited to the particularities of local cultural politics but is explicitly tethered to the larger national context fueled by the backlash to ongoing struggles toward racial (as well as gender and sexual) justice and equality. The text's privileging of LaRocca and its pronounced ethnic inflection—"Sicilian Jazz"—on a Louisiana state-endorsed historical marker reinforces a mythologized view of LaRocca—whom Gennari refers to as one of "jazz's anti-heroes"—that continues to inform and shape how some Italian Americans and others think about and experience the country's cultural history.

One cannot read this marker without considering the changes in New Orleans and throughout the country around public monuments and memorials in recent times. In 2017, then mayor Mitch Landrieu's administration, led by African American and Black Lives Matter activists, removed three monuments erected to traitors to the Union—President Jefferson Davis (dedicated 1911) and the generals Robert E. Lee (dedicated 1884) and P.G.T. Beauregard (dedicated 1915)—which embodied and advanced the myth of the Lost Cause at the service of segregationists. The Lost Cause's counternarrative to the ignoble defeat of seditious enslavers elaborated a redemptive and moralistic rhetoric that glorified the defenders of an idealized Southern antebellum society, expunged slavery as the war's mainspring, and championed white supremacy (see Cox 2012, 15–20). In addition, an obelisk commemorating the violent municipal coup-d'état in 1874 by a terrorist racist organization, the Crescent City White League, was also carted away (see Upton 2015, 50–65). While the small-scale, text-driven placard about a working-class electrician and trumpet player does not compare with the colossal representations of slavers, seditionists, and insurrectionists, nonetheless the imprimatur of a historical marker on the public landscape exults and by extension perpetuates LaRocca's racist and segregationist beliefs as embedded history. The sign's truncated vagueness—the perfunctory language of seven declarative sentences—reconfigures history in the present by rejecting nuance and critical examination as found in Gennari's interpretive account. Monuments, memorials, and markers are not history, with all its messiness and contradictions, but rather idealized renderings of the past, what Kirk Savage calls "self-justifying fables" (2018, xiii), imbued with the attitudes and concerns of the present.

The presence of such a marker devalues and effaces the prevailing condemnation of LaRocca's ludicrous and contemptible pronouncements in the name of ethnic pride. The placard takes a public stand on how Italian American identity is articulated in relationship to the city's fellow citizens within a power dynamic of racialized history that is being examined anew and vigorously challenged in the city and across the country and as such can be seen as an abdication of shared responsibility to others. Laura Ruberto and I have written elsewhere about monuments, memorials, and other commemorative spaces of Italian diasporic impulse: "Awareness of the historical and contemporary ways Italians, broadly defined, have been positioned within various countries' racialized hierarchies of oppression are particularly relevant in our times given the rise of virulent xenophobia, increased nationalism, border restrictions, and racist violence all emerging as part of public rhetoric, individual acts, and government policies" (2022, 7).

Perhaps it should come as no surprise that the LaRocca marker was installed in 2020, at the very moment the country was experiencing a "loud articulation of whiteness," what Matthew Frye Jacobson labels *Confederate* ("Between Race and Ethnicity" 2021), conspicuously manifested in the legislative, litigious, and at times violent defense of public statuary associated with colonialism, white supremacy, and other forms of oppression.[4] In this regard, the plaque's placement at the corner of Esplanade and Decatur is a historically constituted act joining Italian ethnicity and a reactionary whiteness that warrants contextualizing.

The marker's sponsor, the Marsala Cultural Fund, is headed by Charles Marsala, a financial adviser and president of the American Italian Federation of the Southeast, a regional ethnic umbrella organization. Marsala, in fact, attended the 2022 symposium at Tulane University and after my presentation approached me to discuss, among other things, the difficulties he had encountered in placing the LaRocca sign in the city. At that time, he claimed that New Orleans mayor Latoya Cantrell's administration rejected having the marker on city property, and as a result he had resorted to seeking and obtaining state approval and placement (the US Mint is on state property). Marsala is a known entity to Crescent City locals, who have identified him as a "history buff" and a "racist politician" (Koronowski 2018) who is "one of New Orleans' most prominent Confederate monument defenders" (MaCCNO 2020). Marsala has supplemented his active campaigning for monuments long associated with white supremacy with his self-published book *Monument Heist: A Story of Race; A Race to the White House* (2021). While the book contains only a passing reference to Marsala's Italian ethnicity (2021, 13), a close reading of its arguments helps situate the creation and installation of the LaRocca marker within the larger context of whiteness and contemporary expressions of Italian ethnicity.

Weighing in at 676 pages, with more than 400 images, including charts, maps, and sundry reproduced documents, the book is a polemic against "The Cult of Myopic Mayors and a partnership of socialist groups to win the White House" (2021, unpaginated front page). The book's main target is Mayor Landrieu, who Marsala claims—based on unattributable hearsay (2021, 83)—removed the city's four monuments as part of a bid for the White House (2021, 2; 90).[5] Ultimately, Marsala's argument for retaining the Jim Crow–era monuments is predicated on notions of heritage and history. It is the heritage of white Southerners and in particular the descendants of those originally responsible for the commemorative works that are deemed most important, that is, "the people whose great, great grandmothers raised the funds along with others to provide a dignified memorial" (2021, 14). Post–Civil War claims to a unique Southern white/Confederate heritage and identity have reemerged with ferocity in the twenty-first century as strategic exertions in defense of vilified public statuary (see Upton 2015, 58–59,

64). African American opposition to those public symbols of white supremacy is not Marsala's concern, and voices of dissent are sublimated into anonymous mobs of "Antifa," Black Lives Matter, and "Take 'em Down groups" (2021, 46).[6]

Regarding history, Marsala seeks to rectify the "'False Narratives'" of the "Noble citizens with noble intentions [who] have been disparaged inaccurately" (2021, 3).[7] His attempted resurrection of the tainted legacies of Lee, Jackson, and Beauregard is based on the notion that monuments to such reprehensible individuals and associated events are analogous to written biographies and published histories comprising the full spectrum of a person's life or a past episode, and not in fact highly selective symbols of artistically crafted public propaganda. Thus, his revisionist contortions transform Lee into "The Man Who Tamed the Mississippi River" (2021, 219), Jackson into "a slave-owner who brought socialism to the plantation system" (2021, 235), and Beauregard into "America's first Civil Rights Activist" (2021, 70). Marsala dismisses the significance of the monuments' historical context and their ideological role in promoting the Lost Cause and the suppression of African Americans' civil rights (2021, 17; 103). In building his case the author refers to the Civil War as "The War of Southern Independence," a term long used by Confederate apologists seeking to reinforce the narrated machinations that states rights was the cause for secession and not slavery.[8] His support of the Battle of Liberty Place Monument, what James Loewen called "the most overt monument to white supremacy in the United States" (2015), is particularly troubling given that the 1891 lynching of eleven acquitted Italian Americans reanimated fundraising for the uncompleted obelisk (Loewen 2015; Powell 2013, 127–128).

Public spaces of commemoration are not benign, neutral sites but are, in fact, charged with ideological intent that, in turn, becomes imbued with ever-shifting meanings and sentiments. Such conflictual permeations are evident in the unsettled interactions with New Orleans's reviled Confederate monuments for more than a century and the LaRocca marker in more recent times (see MaCCNO 2020). Such works are testaments to the country's unresolved relationship with the legacy of Black resistance to white supremacy. The horrors of chattel slavery, Jim Crow terrorism, and contemporary mass incarceration and police brutality resonate from the now dethroned bronze visages and the newly minted lettering stamped in relief. The twenty-first-century marker heralds LaRocca, an embittered man whose insecurities positioned him in accordance with a racist system of oppression and political disenfranchisement. The promotion of the now discredited trumpeter, coupled with the defense of traitorous enslavers, cannot be dismissed as simple expressions of ethnic pride but should be seen as an example of discernable complicity with systemic racism perpetuated by white folks, with or without vowels at the end of their surnames. Engaging in this brand of advocacy in a city made infamous by the extrajudicial killings of Italian Americans shows a dissonant disregard for the history of racialized prejudice and xenophobic discrimination. In the end, ethnic-inflected apologias for racism like the LaRocca marker are a prime example of the failure of empathy and accountability that John Gennari seeks to rectify with his virtuoso essay.

## Acknowledgment

I thank Stephen Cerulli, Siân Gibby, Laura E. Ruberto, Nick Spitzer, and Anthony Julian Tamburri for their insightful comments to a previous iteration of this essay.

## Notes

[1] This essay is a revised and expanded version of my oral reply to Gennari's keynote given at "The Italian Immigrant Experience: Between Black and White" symposium, Tulane University, September 23, 2022.

[2] Another LaRocca marker exists at the Jazz Walk of Fame in New Orleans at Algiers Point.

[3] The idea that Louis Prima, author of the 1937 song "Sing, Sing, Sing," was "instrumental in introducing swing music," is a grave distortion of the historical record.

[4] See, for example, President Donald Trump's 2020 presidential Executive Order on Protecting American Monuments, Memorials, and Statues and Combating Recent Criminal Violence and the 2017 Unite the Right rally in Charlottesville, Virginia, in defense of a Lee monument the city planned to remove. Florida Governor Ron DeSantis has amplified this reactionary position by legislating control over the ways in which subjects of US history like slavery and the Civil Rights movement, as well as gender identity and sexual orientation, are taught in the state's school system.

[5] The politicized nature of this harangue is notable given Marsala's own political ambitions: Marsala bills himself as the "former mayor of Atherton, California" on the book's cover. In addition to his brief 2005–2006 mayoralty, Marsala ran unsuccessfully as a Republican for US senator of Louisiana in 2016 and for state representative in 2023.

[6] Marsala briefly mentions an African American woman who in 2017 supported, while holding aloft a Confederate battle flag, the maintenance of the Davis monument as if to discredit the Black opposition to the statue's historical white supremacist valence (2021, 156–162).

[7] Despite the book's pretense as a historically grounded work, it is not surprising, given the author's background in business and politics rather than history, that it is bereft of basic scholarly documentation. Despite these omissions Marsala states (2021, 16) that the reproduced documents found in the 192 pages of the twenty-seven appendices (from an 1874 Congressional Report to a 2017 "Lead in Water Report") constitute backing for his various contentions. Occasional spot checking of questionable statements lacking direct citations all too often reveals less than rigorous research practices. One particularly egregious error is Marsala's assertion that New York City's Columbus Monument erected in 1892 was in direct response to the 1891 extrajudicial killing of eleven Italian Americans in New Orleans (2021, 46; 385–386).

[8] Marsala's justification for using this loaded term is that the war's cause was due to the South's "grievances with the Union starting with the banking system conflicts in 1811, state's rights on tariffs and taxation in 1816, and whether to abolish, expand, end by manumission, or retain slavery starting in 1830" (2021, 34n.1).

## Works Cited

"Between Race and Ethnicity: Greek-America in the Times of Black Lives Matter." 2021. Hellenic Studies Program at Yale. March 22. YouTube video. https://youtu.be/V4vGAuoT4wY.

Cox, Karen L. 2021. *No Common Ground: Confederate Monuments and the Ongoing Fight for Racial Justice.* Chapel Hill: The University of North Carolina Press.

Fleegler, Robert L. 2013. *Ellis Island Nation: Immigration Policy and American Identity in the Twentieth Century.* Philadelphia: University of Pennsylvania Press.

Harney, Robert F. 1993. "Caboto and Other Parentela: The Uses of the Italian Canadian Past." In *From the Shores of Hardship: Italians in Canada. Essays by Robert F. Harney*, edited by Nicholas De Maria Harney, 1–27. Lewiston, NY: Éditions Soleil Publishing.

Koronowski, Ryan. 2018. "Republican Congresswoman Met with Racist Politician Who Thinks Jefferson Davis Empowered Slaves." *ThinkProgress* Nov 2. https://archive.thinkprogress.org/claudia-tenney-met-politician-who-thinks-jefferson-davis-empowered-slaves-3e7a647260b5/.

Loewen, James. 2015. "The Monument to White Power that Still Stands in New Orleans." September 3. https://historynewsnetwork.org/blog/153667.

MaCCNO (Music and Culture Coalition of New Orleans). 2020, "How a New Historic Marker Creates a Literal Link to White Supremacy in the French Quarter." *Antigravity*. November. https://antigravitymagazine.com/column/how-a-historic-marker-and-attached-qr-code-create-a-literal-link-to-white-supremacy-in-the-french-quarter/.

Marsala, Charles. *Monument Heist: A Story of Race; A Race to the White House.* 2021. eBookIt.com.

Powell, Lawrence N. 2013. "Reinventing Tradition: Liberty Place, Historical Memory, and Silk-stocking Vigilantism in New Orleans Politics" In *From Slavery to Emancipation in the Atlantic World*, edited by Sylvia R. Frey and Betty Wood, 127–149. New York: Routledge.

Ruberto, Laura E. and Joseph Sciorra. 2022. "Disrupted and Unsettled: An Introduction to Monuments, Memorials, and Italian Migrations" *Italian American Review* 12.1 (Winter), 1–35.

Savage, Kirk. 2018. *Standing Soldiers, Kneeling Slaves: Race, War, and Monument in Nineteenth-Century America.* Princeton: Princeton University Press.

Upton, Dell. 2015. *What Can and Can't Be Said: Race, Uplift, and Monument Building in the Contemporary South.* New Haven: Yale University Press.

# Index

www.ingramcontent.com/pod-product-compliance
Lightning Source LLC
Chambersburg PA
CBHW081400270326
41930CB00015B/3366